Good News People

Recognizing Diocesan Evangelists

Good News People

Recognizing Diocesan Evangelists

A report of a Working Party
of the
House of Bishops

 CHURCH HOUSE
PUBLISHING

Church House Publishing
Church House
Great Smith Street
London
SW1P 3NZ

ISBN 0 7151 5544 X

A report of a Working Party of the House of Bishops

Published 1999 for the Board of Mission of the Church of England by
Church House Publishing

*This report has only the authority of the working party which produced it. It has
been approved by the House of Bishops.*

Cover design by Tain Oliff, Image-On Artworks

Printed in England by Halstan & Co. Ltd

Contents

Members of the
House of Bishops' Working Party

Chairman: The Rt Revd John Finney, former Bishop of Pontefract

Members: The Revd Peter Bowers, Rural Dean of Dover

The Revd Dr Arnold Browne, Fellow and Dean of Chapel, Trinity College, Cambridge

Mr Martin Cavender, Director of Springboard

The Rt Revd Richard Garrard, Bishop of Penrith

Dr Janet Hodgson, Adviser in Local Mission, Durham Diocese

The Revd Dr Derek Tidball, Principal of London Bible College

Mrs Hilary Unwin, Accredited Lay Worker in the Diocese of Oxford and Diocesan Adviser for Lay Ministry

Secretary: The Revd Canon Philip King, General Secretary of the Board of Mission

Minutes Secretary: Dr John Ledger, Reader and Project Manager for Lambeth Palace Millennium Opening.

The Brief of the Working Party

1. To examine the use of evangelists in the New Testament and in church history; in particular their relation to other ministries in the Church;

2. to examine the issues regarding office, order and recognition in relation to evangelists. It will pay particular regard to the Office of Evangelist at present represented mainly, if not entirely, by those commissioned as officers in the Church Army;

3. to examine and evaluate the existing and proposed diocesan patterns for selecting, training, assessing, supporting and using evangelists;

4. to discover and evaluate models from other churches and other parts of the Anglican Communion;

5. to produce recommendations and guidelines for dioceses regarding:

   > criteria and procedures for the selection of evangelists;

   > methods for training evangelists (including a list of those courses, etc. currently available);

   > a suggested Code of Conduct for evangelists;

   > the use of evangelists within a diocese;

   > accountability and continuing support;

   > the place of the bishop in the process;

6. to liaise with the College of Evangelists Implementation Group in order to enable evangelists who have some form of diocesan recognition to gain national recognition if required.

Foreword

By the Chairman of the House of Bishops

Perhaps one of the great discoveries we have made as a Church in the 1990s – the Decade of Evangelism – is that evangelism is at the heart of what the Church is and what it stands for. If the Church is not an outward-looking, Christ-promoting body, it falls far short of its Founder's wishes. Within the Church as a whole there are gifted people who have specific evangelistic gifts. For some people, however, the word 'evangelist' has negative associations. This report describes the real people – ordinary, humble men and women of God who sensitively and carefully want to share their faith with others. I am delighted that so many dioceses are seeing how such people can be more fully recognized in their life. Some are being used primarily in their own parishes, others in a wider ministry.

For many years the Church Army has been invaluable in providing trained and effective evangelists to the life of the Church. However, it is particularly appropriate at the end of the Decade of Evangelism that this report commending the use of other, local evangelists should be published. It gives clear guidance to those who are thinking of some form of official recognition. The report takes its place alongside the report that set up the College of Evangelists for those whose ministry is wider than a single diocese.

Rightly the report examines the place of the evangelist in the Bible and Christian history before coming to its conclusions on the meaning of the word 'evangelist' and the way in which potential evangelists can be selected, trained, recognized and used.

I would like to thank the members of the Working Party who produced the report.

✠ GEORGE CANTUAR
Archbishop of Canterbury
July 1999

Introduction

By the Chairman of the Working Party

Few working parties live up to their name. Although we have only had five meetings a great deal of work has been done by members of the House of Bishops' Working Party between meetings, and pairs of us have visited six dioceses.

For all of us it has been a voyage of exploration. To our surprise we found that very little theological work has been done on the nature of the evangelist's ministry in the New Testament and even less on the place of the evangelist in Christian history. We hope that the work that we have begun will be taken further by others.

The intention of the working party was not merely to look at what had been done and examine some of the issues that arise, but also to be of practical help to those dioceses which may wish to consider this ministry within their own life. The final section is therefore called 'Questions for Further Consideration', which suggests how dioceses and others can take this further if they so wish.

Throughout our work we have been aware of the contribution of other denominations and the presence of the Revd Dr Derek Tidball, Principal of the London Bible College, has been most fruitful. We are aware that several denominations in the UK are also examining how they can honour and integrate the evangelist within their own traditions and await this report with interest. Some areas of the Anglican Communion have for many years also recognized the contribution of evangelists and we have sought to learn from them, but we are also aware that other parts of the Anglican Communion are also examining their own practice.

Where the Church of England is concerned we are conscious that the present approach to the work of the evangelist is comparatively recent and we have sought to stake a very tender sapling rather than prop up a grown tree. Inevitably and rightly at this stage we have been tentative and have therefore included few 'Recommendations' but we have given many indications of where the future might lie. Apart from the long-established and focused work of the Church Army, the Church of England is only now beginning to discover and use the gifts of the evangelist in its diocesan and parochial strategies. We hope that this report will lead to a right use of a ministry that functions on the boundary and that seeks to interpret the gospel to the world and the world to the church.

We would wish to thank the House of Bishops for setting us this fascinating task and trust the report will further discussion rather than end it.

✠ JOHN FINNEY

The former Bishop of Pontefract

CHAPTER 1

The Evangelist in the Past

1.1   Where does the evangelist fit into the life of the Church? It is not a new question. It was debated with some vigour in the nineteenth century at the time when the Office of Lay Reader was being established. In 1896 The Upper House of Canterbury appointed a committee 'to consider what steps may be taken to give a general recognition to the Order of Lay Evangelists founded in the diocese of Lichfield and similar organisations, and to extend and develop such work throughout the Church under episcopal authority and control'. There were four evangelistic agencies seeking recognition at the time: of the four only the Church Army (founded in 1882) has survived and flourished.

1.2   The result of the debate was that evangelists should be classed with Lay Readers. In 1898 the Convocations of Canterbury resolved 'that it is expedient, in order to recognize a trained Evangelist, and authorise him to perform the duties of his office in any Diocese, that the Bishop of the Diocese should grant him a "Reader's" licence in a form similar to that recommended by the Bishops in 1866'. It is clear that they were thinking of 'men who belong to the people' who were to be paid as evangelists.

1.3   The lumping together of Lay Readers and Evangelists was much resented and in 1952 the Central Reader's Conference made strong representations that they should be separated, largely on the grounds that the work of a Reader was voluntary while evangelists were paid. This led to the passing of Canon E 7.2 by which those admitted to the Office of Evangelist were thereby 'admitted as a lay worker of the Church'.

1.4   In practice this has meant that the officers of the Church Army have been the only officially recognized evangelists in the Church of England. However, there has been one exception: in the 1950s the Bishop of Coventry, Cuthbert Bardsley, commissioned one man to the Office of

Evangelist who was not a member of the Church Army – it may or may not be a significant exception and we examine the position of Church Army officers and the possibility of widening the office to include others in Chapter 4.

1.5   Besides the Church Army there have been a number of different organizations that have evangelists. Some are interdenominational bodies while others are specifically Anglican, such as the evangelists employed by the Church Pastoral Aid Society.

1.6   Still others have been employed by dioceses as sector ministers – sometimes they have been directly evangelistic in their work while others have been advisers of the diocese and parishes. Collectively they have been called 'Diocesan Missioners', and they have their own long-established network connected to the General Synod Board of Mission. However, different dioceses call the post by different names, five of them using the term 'Diocesan Evangelist'. It should be noted that this report does not concern itself with these sector ministers, or with the wider apostolic ministry that is peculiar to the order of bishops.

1.7   From time to time individual parishes, or in a few cases teams or deaneries, have employed evangelists as a contribution to their ministry in their area.

1.8   Many religious communities have mission written into their constitutions and have engaged in evangelistic work in one form or another. The Working Party contacted several and found that, although they wished to exercise their evangelistic ministry, they saw it primarily as the work of the whole community rather than of individuals, and were not therefore looking for some form of recognition.

1.9   There have been certain important similarities that have linked the above groups of people:

- most of them have been stipendiary (or have received sustenance from a religious order) and have filled certain posts for which they have been trained and to which they have been appointed;

- they have been both ordained and lay;

- they have been recognized in some way, though the style of this recognition has varied considerably. While all Church Army officers have been admitted to the Office of an Evangelist, others have been licensed to work in a diocese or parish. Others have had less formal recognition by virtue of their employment by an organization or church.

1.10   Besides these there are considerable numbers of individuals whose evangelistic ministry is recognized and used both inside and outside their parishes. Some belong to one of the religious orders. Some belong to the Fellowship of Parish Evangelism – a flourishing voluntary Anglican organization with a current membership of 231. In the light of our recommendation regarding the importance of acknowledging the evangelistic ministry of clergy it is noteworthy that 133 of them are ordained. Few of them are paid as evangelists (mainly those who are Church Army captains). Some see their evangelistic work as the main part of their ministry, while for others it is confined to taking part in occasional missions.

1.11   However, in recent years (certainly since the 1980s) there has been a growing wish to have people recognized as evangelists who are not necessarily paid by a parish or diocese or linked closely with a voluntary organization. The encouragement and growth of lay ministry within the Church and the wish for training by many individuals has led to a call for evangelists to be both trained and recognized. The subject was of sufficient importance for the House of Bishops to ask ACCM to set up a working group under the chairmanship of the Bishop of Gloucester in the early 1980s. It is important to note that the group was asked to report on the Office of Evangelist – it did not consider other forms of recognition. The report offered four options to the Church:

- abolish the Office of Evangelist;

- discourage further entry, steering future applicants into other recognized ministries (Deacon, Accredited Lay Worker or Reader);

- keep the Office as a separate lay ministry within the church open to laypeople other than members of the Church Army;

- extend the Office to both lay and ordained people.

The Gloucester Report was certain that the present situation was anomalous, but could not recommend abolition. It hoped that a consensus would emerge at a later date. The report was presented to the council of ACCM in November 1985 and to the House of Bishops in June 1986. It was decided not to publish it.

1.12   The advent of the Decade of Evangelism raised the issue again and another group was set up, this time with representation from the Board of Mission, the Board of Education, ABM and the Church Army. It should be noted that the remit of this group was to examine ways of giving recognition to 'National Evangelists' – a comparatively small number of people for whom nationally recognized accreditation would be useful to their ministry. Their report made an important advance by speaking of 'recognition' rather than thinking more narrowly of the Order of Evangelists. It proposed setting up a 'College of Evangelists' whose members would have an active evangelistic ministry wider than a diocese and who had been through a selection procedure before being accepted for membership. A board for this college has now been established under the chairmanship of the Bishop of Southampton and the first members of the college will be recognized in 1999.

1.13   This report (BOM 12/94) was sent to all diocesan bishops for their comment in 1995 and was discussed in the House of Bishops. Although there were many caveats, there were only four dioceses that were not actively interested in the idea. More than that, the Bishops went further than the brief given to the authors of BOM 12/94 and commented that the growing desire for diocesan evangelists should also be taken into consideration.

1.14   As a result, the House of Bishops Standing Committee in May 1996 asked the Archbishops to establish a Diocesan Evangelists Working Party to examine the current position regarding diocesan evangelists and produce recommendations and guidelines for the future.

1.15   The need for further thought on the subject was underlined by two conferences organized by the Board of Mission to discuss diocesan evangelists and discover what was happening in the dioceses. The first conference, in 1995, was comparatively small but showed that four or five dioceses were pressing ahead with differing models of diocesan evangelists. The second conference, in 1997, was far larger and was attended by representatives of over 20 dioceses: it was clear that a considerable number were either establishing some form of recognition of evangelists or were thinking of doing so.

1.16   It is clear from these conferences and from other evidence that several forms of recognition of diocesan evangelists are being experimented with.

(a) **Recognition of an existing ministry**

Some dioceses are identifying existing evangelists who are already seen as having an evangelistic ministry and then giving them some form of recognition (usually from the bishop). Their training is individually geared to their previous experience and knowledge.

This pattern means that comparatively few people are recognized, but they have their ministry affirmed and may be used across parish boundaries more easily since diocesan recognition commends their ministry and shows that it can be received safely. It is also possible to indicate to parishes the areas of work in which the evangelist is most skilled, e.g. pubs and clubs, outdoor work, young people, etc.

This is sometimes called the Southwell pattern since it was in that diocese that a Letter of Commendation from the diocesan bishop was first given to a few individuals who had already been widely used in the diocese.

(b) **Training for potential ministry**

Other dioceses are setting up training programmes to encourage people to learn about evangelism and to give them practical experience of this ministry. Some courses are fairly academic and run alongside

Readers' training while others are more experiential and emphasize reflection on the evangelism that the trainees have experienced.

This pattern tends to produce a larger number of evangelists, working mainly in their own parish but beyond it on occasion. It is often called the Rochester pattern after the diocese that pioneered it.

(c) **Collaborative**

This pattern of ministry is based upon people working together, usually in locally based teams. At present many dioceses are setting up 'local ministry teams', sometimes allied with Ordained Local Ministers. In such cases evangelists are part of the team and may train alongside others.

This collaborative style of ministry for evangelists has been less in evidence in the dioceses so far though many feel that it has much to commend it for the future as more ministry teams become established. As will be seen in the next chapter we have evidence that this is already happening. However, it does not provide all the answers since evangelists may well be present in parishes where no such collaborative ministry is in place.

It should be noted that these different approaches are not mutually exclusive. For example, it would be possible for a diocese to have a few evangelists used across the diocese while at the same time training others for use primarily in their own parish and also encouraging still others to be members of their local ministry team (where one was in place).

1.17   Where individuals have shown considerable evangelistic gifts and are beginning to be used outside their diocese then their bishop can propose them as possible members of the national College of Evangelists. It is usually expected that he or she will have been a diocesan evangelist for three years before being suitable for consideration as a potential member of the college (this rule will be relaxed in the early days of the existence of the college).

1.18 It should be noted that we have used the term 'diocesan evangelist' to describe those who are exercising an evangelistic ministry in parishes and dioceses because that was the one used in our brief. In practice they are often called by some other term, as can be seen in the next chapter.

1.19 We found that the different words used to denote the affirmation of a person's ministry were used with different meanings and this caused confusion. The situation is discussed in detail in Chapter 4 ('The words used to describe affirmation within the Church'), but it may be helpful to note that we use the term 'recognition' throughout the report as a general word to describe such affirmation. Thus, recognition might be by ordination, a letter from the bishop, commissioning, licensing, etc.

CHAPTER 2

The Present Position

2.1   The working party was set up because of the growing number of dioceses that were establishing some method of recognizing the ministry of the evangelist (whether working mainly at diocesan, deanery or parish level) and the even larger number of dioceses that were examining the possibility of doing this.

We set ourselves to find out how widespread this was. We did this through a questionnaire sent to every diocese and by visits to six dioceses and through many informal conversations.

The questionnaire

2.2   The questionnaire was sent to all dioceses in November 1997 asking them about their thinking on the subject and, if they were recognizing evangelists, the process of selection, training and support that they had established. It was a considerable inquisition and we are grateful to the bishops and others who completed it.

2.3   The position at the end of 1997 is summarized below from the 32 diocesan responses. More recent contacts suggest that more dioceses are looking carefully at the subject and, in some cases, seeking to recognize some form of diocesan evangelist.

(a) **The numbers involved**

Fourteen dioceses had discussed the idea, sometimes informally. Three of these had decided to go no further, though some of these knew of people who were looking for some sort of recognition. It was clearly still at the experimental level for most dioceses: for example, Chichester has appointed a new Diocesan Missioner whose job description asks him to look at the possibility of having diocesan evangelists. Only Southwell and Rochester had had schemes in place for more than five years – most had just started or were about to start.

As a result the number of evangelists who had been recognized was comparatively small. Rochester had 40, Southwell had seven, and most of the rest were in single figures. However, there were larger numbers in training in some of the dioceses. Thus, Sheffield had more than 25 either recognized or in training.

(b) The meaning of 'evangelist'

In those dioceses that had some form of recognition, their definitions of 'evangelist' tended to emphasize the effective communication of the gospel as being central to the ministry of an evangelist. Some examples of the definitions of an evangelist are as follows:

> Someone who has the proven gifts and calling to evangelise through word and action outside the networks of their daily life. (Wakefield)

> A man or woman gifted by God in drawing people to a living faith in Jesus Christ. (Chester)

> One who has the gift of drawing together the fragments of Christian Witness and experience and helping people to know that they are personally loved and called by God . . . a midwife to Christian faith. (Hereford)

> A person who is gifted and anointed by God to the work of proclaiming the good news such that people come to faith in the Lord Jesus Christ as a result of their ministry. (Winchester Director of Faith Development)

It was very noticeable that most dioceses made the assumption that this was to be a 'lay' ministry.

(c) **The place of ministry**

The place in which the evangelists exercised their ministry varied: roughly a third of dioceses saw them as working only in their parish, a third saw them as working mainly in diocese or deanery and the other third as having a ministry both within and outside the parish.

Their title often reflected this – some dioceses called them diocesan evangelists, while others described them as parish evangelists (and a few had deanery evangelists). Several dioceses preferred to call them 'mission enablers', 'outreach coordinators', 'mission advisers', etc.

(d) **Selection**

Most of the lay candidates came forward with the recommendation of their parish and/or the Diocesan Missioner, or, in one case, the Diocesan Director of Ordinands.

A degree of self-selection is apparent in some dioceses. Some of those that have a three year training programme allow the candidates themselves to choose, after consultation, the path they think is appropriate at the end of their second year.

What was looked for in a candidate depended on the diocesan view of the ministry. Those that saw the recognition of an existing ministry as the most important factor naturally looked for an effective past ministry in evangelism. Those that sought to train potential evangelists looked for possible rather than proven ability but asked that they should have 'a heart for evangelism' (Lichfield).

(e) **Churchmanship**

There was some evidence that there is some weighting of the candidates towards the evangelical end of the spectrum. However, it was not as evident as might have been expected. One diocese described all its candidates as 'middling' and others had evangelists from a catholic background. Similarly, by no means all of them would describe themselves as charismatic – one diocese said none of its candidates came from that stable.

(f) **Training**

Once again the amount and content of the training depended on the diocesan view of the evangelistic ministry. Where candidates were already expected to have a track record in evangelism they were required only to add those skills that were needed – some using a Church Army course. Often these candidates had had previous formal training – some were already licensed as Readers. However, where they were seen as potential rather than as actual evangelists they were given a full training. Often this followed a pattern akin to that required of Readers though usually with a greater emphasis on practical experience and reflection.

It was noticeable that those dioceses that were moving towards the recognition of parochial teams (with or without OLMs) were beginning to train evangelists alongside the other members of the team, but this was too new for it to have become established.

(g) **Recognition**

There was considerable variation in practice:

- by letter of commendation (Wakefield and Southwell);
- by certificate (Rochester, Manchester);
- by bishop's licence (Rochester, Southwell);
- by commissioning (Lichfield).

Often there was a special service where the evangelists were recognized formally. This might be conducted by the diocesan, or it might be delegated to a suffragan bishop, an Archdeacon, DDO or Diocesan Missioner. Even if he was not present he signed any licence, letter of commendation, etc.

(h) Job description

This was comparatively rare. Leicester expected one to be drawn up between the evangelist and the diocese, while Rochester and Exeter had one with the parish.

(i) Accountability

In four dioceses the evangelist was accountable primarily to his or her parish priest and in two to the Diocesan Missioner.

Use of mentor: it was required in Rochester that each evangelist should have a spiritual director and Wakefield asked the Diocesan Missioner to act as mentor to the diocesan evangelists.

(j) Difficulties

Most of the evangelists who have been recognized find that they are fully used in their parish and outside. Indeed for some of those with a ministry wider than the parish care had to be taken that they were not overextended. Difficulties are reported when there is a change of incumbent and he or she is unable to appreciate or make full use of the ministry of the evangelist. However, another issue was mentioned that is common to Readers and others called to training for a lay ministry. When a PCC and incumbent agree that a layperson should go forward for training, a period of up to three years can pass before they are recognized. During this time they may well have to withdraw somewhat from the life of the parish in order to fulfil the demands of the training. By the time they have finished they may well be faced by a new incumbent and a PCC with considerably changed personnel.

However, despite some difficulties all the dioceses we encountered found that, overall, their recognition of the ministry of the evangelist was helpful. As Rochester said, 'In our experience the evangelists are some of the most hopeful and encouraging folk being trained and used in the diocese today. They are quite well established and have been greatly appreciated in their work in the parish.'

The visits

2.4   Members of the working party are most grateful for the energy and thoughtful preparation that dioceses put into these visits and that made them so helpful to the working party. We deliberately chose to visit dioceses where the idea of Diocesan Evangelists had been looked at and rejected as well as those where the idea had been accepted.

In order to respect the openness of those we met and to enable us to report more fully the dioceses are not named.

2.5   DIOCESE A

Primarily rural.

2.6   The diocese had a considerable commitment to collaborative ministry through its Local Ministry Scheme. It felt that in the small communities that were most representative of the diocese it was important to ensure that all members of the teams were thinking evangelistically and that the training process mirrored this desire. There were therefore no diocesan evangelists as such, although an individual might specialize as a team's 'standard-bearer' for evangelism. Indeed, there was some resistance to the idea of individuals being called 'evangelists' as a 'label for life' in communities where existing relationships were likely to be more important than new roles.

2.7   Training in mission and evangelism is integral to all Local Ministry Development: one of the training units states, 'evangelism belongs to and is the calling of the whole Church. It is the proclamation of the word, the living out in deed and the symbolisation in sacrament of the Christian faith and hope.' Stipendiary clergy and deployable NSMs were seen as having an oversight role in an area and were expected to establish evangelistic priorities within it.

2.8   DIOCESE B

Primarily based on a single city but with considerable industrialized areas outside the city and with some small rural parishes.

2.9   The bishop sees evangelism as the essence of a living church and seeks to develop an 'ethos' for evangelism. There is currently a review of diocesan life, including the Diocesan Evangelists.

2.10   There has been a diocesan programme for selecting and training evangelists for five years and there are now more than 30 evangelists recognized or in training. We found an excellent sense of community among the evangelists, who receive support from each other as well as from the diocesan officer concerned.

2.11   Some began to think of training as an evangelist through the Walk of 600 Men but most came through parish recommendation. About half the evangelists said that they had had a strong sense of 'inner call' and the others that they had begun because they had been invited by others to consider this ministry. A 'Shop Window' day is held at diocesan level at which people can learn about the different forms of lay ministry possible. If an individual wishes to begin training, his or her PCC is asked for its opinion and for some finance to support the candidacy. The diocese is responsible for conducting the interview and for the decision as to whether an individual should receive training. It was noted that there was a degree of self-selection during training as some dropped out.

After selection a Parish Link Group is set up to keep close relationships with the home parish. Incumbents who have trainee evangelists are involved throughout the training (and it was suggested that other members of the home parish might also be involved to prevent the sense of alienation that can occur).

2.12   In one group of evangelists none described themselves as evangelical, four as charismatic, eight as 'middling' and one as Anglo-Catholic. In personality tests most rated as introvert.

2.13   Training was for two years under the guidance of the Course Management Group. A deliberate attempt had been made to make the course accessible to those with little education – there were no essays but assignments were demanding and there was much reflection on the context of evangelism and on work carried out.

There was some pressure to make the course more academic in tone, but the evangelists themselves found its great strength was that it was 'a practical course', and wanted it to be even more so. The Church Army courses were used. The requirement was about 80 hours of training each year. The importance of having experience of other parishes and contexts was mentioned by many of the evangelists as one of the most helpful elements in the course.

2.14   Recognition was through admission at a service in the cathedral and authorization (not licensing) in their parish for three years. It had been found that this authorization gave a greater sense of confidence and willingness to train and lead others in the parish.

2.15   A Ministry Agreement is drawn up between the evangelist and the parish in which he or she will be working. Evangelists can begin work in the parish some six months before authorization and this is seen as part of the training process. They were encouraged to have a spiritual director/mentor.

2.16   A meeting with incumbents who have diocesan evangelists showed how widely they were being used. Leading nurture courses, baptism preparation, visiting old people's homes and other routines of parish life were being undertaken as well as work outside the life of the church in house-to-house visiting, working in pubs, hospital chaplaincy, youth evangelism, etc. Several were involved in church plants.

2.17   Accountability was through the parish priest and the Warden of Evangelists who had triennial ministry reviews with each evangelist. The warden saw his work as pastoral but also disciplinary if required. Some of his time had been spent helping new incumbents to make appropriate use of their evangelists.

2.18 DIOCESE C

A diocese with considerable rural areas but also many urban areas that bear the scars of heavy industry.

2.19   The diocese had struggled with the right title to give their 'diocesan evangelists'. They had started with 'Evangelism Enabler' and then moved to 'Outreach Leader' and eventually to 'Outreach Coordinator'. There was some impatience with dealing with close definitions of evangelism or evangelist since it could prevent the apostolic ministry of the church being done. Nevertheless the diocese put considerable emphasis on their Outreach Coordinators being people who would 'enable outreach and make evangelism happen in the parish' by helping the congregation to evangelize, rather than those who would 'do' evangelism for the parish, though it was clear that they were involved in hands-on evangelism themselves. An Outreach Coordinator was defined as 'an enabler, encourager and motivator in leading people to Christ'.

2.20   Training is through a Local Ministry Scheme in which all students take the Bishop's Certificate during the first two years. After completing this students divide for a further year's training as Reader, Pastoral Carer, Spirituality or Social Responsibility Leader or Outreach Coordinator (some might also go on to ordination). At the end of the first year of the Bishop's Certificate students discuss their future with their course tutor and with their PCC. There was a strong tendency for people to choose to become a Reader, 'because everyone knows what a Reader is'. For people who were allowed to take the Outreach Coordinator's third year some proven ability was looked for and the main call came from the parish itself, which called people out to the various ministries in the Parish Leadership Team. At least one of the three terms of the final year would include practical experience of evangelism.

2.21   It was assumed that there would be a working agreement drawn up between the incumbent and the Outreach Coordinator. Further support had not yet been fully worked out.

2.22   The Evangelism Track has only recently become a possibility and the first two Outreach Coordinators have only just started work in their parishes so it is too early to say what their overall impact will be.

2.23   DIOCESE D
A very rural diocese with some towns and urban areas.

2.24   This diocese has looked closely at the possibility of diocesan evangelists and decided that it was not appropriate for them in their context of mainly small villages.

2.25   While clergy numbers have declined in the diocese, the number of Readers has doubled, as has the number of Local Ministry Teams. This 'collegiate' model is felt to be right in the social context where it was important to give people 'permission' to minister. The growth of such ministry has been such that questions of oversight, appraisal and monitoring are becoming important.

2.26   In the rural context having a label is difficult – 'It is bad enough being a GP – to be licensed as a Reader is problematic.' For this reason a 'collegiate' model was more appropriate as the concept of the team is more easily accepted. The title of 'evangelist' would be deeply off-putting, though there was the possibility of drawing people with evangelistic gifts into the parish team. Evangelism was increasingly being seen in terms of spiritual direction – helping a person to find God and then to move on to maturity.

2.27   There was felt to be considerable resistance to major evangelistic campaigns – 'like a juggernaut full of food arriving, just as we are developing a team to help people with subsistence farming'.

2.28   DIOCESE E
A diocese with few rural areas and much post-industrial dereliction.

2.29   It was felt important to make the fullest use of the evangelistic gifts that existed in the diocese by encouraging evangelism in the parish, but also to have a few evangelists with a proven track record who could be available for work throughout the diocese.

2.30 A major early stimulus had been the invitation by a deanery in another diocese to carry out a mission. A team of 250 people, led by the diocesan bishop, went on the mission and they came back determined to evangelize in their own parishes. It also showed that there were a few people who were particularly gifted and whose talents needed a wider canvas than their own parish.

2.31 Three people were then invited to consider the possibility of becoming Diocesan Evangelists by the Diocesan Missioner and were interviewed by the suffragan bishop. Each then had a training package prepared for them individually. After completion of this they were then given a Bishop's Letter of Commendation at a public occasion at the end of 1997.

2.32 It was noteworthy that one of the three Diocesan Evangelists works mainly through clowning and another is profoundly deaf. It is intended to expand the number in the near future, and it is not restricted to laypeople.

2.33 DIOCESE F

A mainly urban diocese with some rural areas.

2.34 In 1988 the diocese looked at the church in Uganda and its pattern for training and using evangelists. They then set up an experimental Diocesan Evangelists scheme, which ran for five years before being made a formal part of the diocesan structure. There are now 32 licensed evangelists and 18 in training. As in Diocese C, it is a lay training pattern in which there is a two-year initial course and then students divide with a third year's more focused training as Readers, Pastoral Assistants, Evangelists, etc.

2.35 No clergy have been recognized as evangelists – possibly because of the African pattern that was the original inspiration.

2.36 The understanding of evangelist which is used is mainly that of a parish mission enabler working 'at the back of the church' – so much so that no training in preaching is given. Indeed, there was so great a desire to avoid the popular image of an evangelist that training in more up front evangelism (being part of a mission team, etc.) was largely absent and some of the evangelists felt they were ill-equipped for this role.

2.37   It was noticeable that the evangelists came from all churchmanships and different personality types ('mouse-like people can blossom in the training'). There was no universally accepted definition of evangelism that would cover the spectrum from outright challenge through to 'care and share'. In fact, there was some realization that the uncertainty can provoke thought – 'disquiet about the word "evangelism" can be helpful'.

2.38   Selection is through the parish, either as a result of personal initiative or as a result of suggestion by other members of the church. The approval of the PCC is required.

2.39   Training is largely modular: the Church Army has contributed considerably to the programme. Most found it helpful and energizing and the overall verdict of one leader was that it 'has gone better than I dared hope'. Each parish pays towards their own trainee evangelist and there is a small amount on the diocesan budget.

2.40   Evangelists are commissioned for three years, renewable after consultation with their parish priest and PCC. They are also members of the Evangelists' Fellowship.

2.41   Accountability is to the parish priest and to the recently appointed Warden of Evangelists. Experience showed that evangelists use a great deal of spiritual energy and quickly become dry unless they are supported.

2.42   While there were difficulties in some parishes because of failure to fit the evangelist into the structure of parish life or because of personality differences, there was a general sense of enthusiasm that the evangelists were a major contribution to the parishes in which they were involved. To prevent the occasional difficulties within a parish there was some call for evangelists to be linked with a deanery, but this was generally felt to break a vital link with the local situation. Difficulties usually occurred where the parish had had little involvement in the training of the evangelist. It also helped if the evangelist was seen as a trainer of people in the parish in evangelism, i.e. his or her skills were accepted and used.

2.43   Some evangelists were finding themselves in situations outside their immediate parish and were looking for training for this wider role.

Conclusions

2.44   THE WORKING PARTY CAME TO THE FOLLOWING CONCLUSIONS:

(a) There is sufficient experience among the dioceses to recognize that diocesan evangelists are in the process of becoming a significant part of the life of a growing number of dioceses, but it is still very early days and only two dioceses can be said to have had evangelists for any length of time. There is widespread interest in the subject and even in those dioceses that have examined the possibility and decided it was inappropriate for them there is a desire to ensure that the evangelistic nature of the church is expressed through individuals.

(b) The different models of selection and training produce very different results – either a few evangelists with a wide brief or a larger number with a more parish-centred ministry. However, there appears to be a shift to a more collaborative style of ministry where the evangelist is a member of the parish team.

(c) There is some resistance to the recognition of diocesan evangelists in the more rural dioceses where it is felt that the community context lends itself to seeing evangelism as a task to be shared by the local team.

(d) It was felt to be most important that the home parish is involved throughout the selection, training and use of the evangelist. A written agreement can be helpful in defining boundaries.

(e) The great majority of evangelists are not being used in 'up-front' evangelism but in work within the parish as visitors, nurture group leaders, etc.

(f) In the training programmes the most applauded elements were those that gave practical experience and the opportunity to reflect upon it. Exposure to unfamiliar situations, e.g. across churchmanships, was also found to be helpful.

(g) The Church Army has played a significant role in a number of dioceses and this work may now be ready to be evaluated and refined.

(h) Many evangelists are being used, not only to evangelize, but to train others to evangelize.

(i) It was noticeable that all the evangelists who have been recognized were lay, and most dioceses saw the training of evangelists as another strand in their lay training schemes. Although some dioceses recognized that clergy might be evangelists they had not recognized any.

(j) There was a disinclination on the part of some dioceses to use the term 'evangelist' and other titles have been devised, though no commonly used alternative has yet come to the fore.

The working party is most grateful to the dioceses who taught us so much. Many of the issues raised and our evaluation of them underlie Chapters 5 and 6 where we discuss possible patterns of selection and training and the questions that need to be addressed.

The local evangelist in other denominations

2.45   A major national or international figure like Billy Graham has long been recognized as an important element in the mission of the church by many nonconformist denominations. However, it is only in recent years that they have been seeking to give greater recognition to the local evangelist within the congregation. The Evangelical Alliance has been working to draw together the initiatives being taken by the Baptists, the United Reformed Church and the Methodists. The working party was in touch with these denominations and with Churches Together in England.

2.46   The Roman Catholic Church works apostolically largely through its Orders. Many of these would see themselves as being engaged in secondary evangelism – refreshing and renewing faith that is lying dormant and in need of revitalizing (often this is done through parish missions and retreats). However, there are a few, such as the Sion Community, which would see themselves as being engaged in primary evangelism – the conversion of those who have not made a profession of faith.

The evangelist in the rest of the Anglican Communion

2.47   In 1984 ACC-6 gave the following as its definition of evangelism.

> The proclamation of the historical, biblical Christ as Saviour and Lord, with a view to persuading people to come to him personally and so be reconciled to God, to one another and to creation. The results of evangelism include obedience to Christ, incorporation into his church, and responsible service to the world. (p. 49)

It also said that every local church should be a missionary church with a programme for evangelism with all members being mobilized for the task of being front-line missionaries, and with clergy enabling and equipping the laity. Those called to be full-time evangelists should be properly trained and the ACC asked for a raising of the status of the evangelist. Because evangelists, like other lay ministers, are perceived in some areas to be inferior, many of them seek ordination to the priesthood. ACC-6 argued for the establishing of an order of full-time evangelists who used methods 'consistent with the ethos of our Anglican heritage'. It spoke scathingly of cheap evangelism, peddling cheap grace as a 'counter-sign of the kingdom' when action is divorced from the preaching of individual salvation. It quoted Orlando Costas, who described such a gospel as proclaiming 'a conscience-soothing Jesus, with an unscandalous cross, an otherworldly kingdom, a private inwardly spirit, a pocket God, a spiritualized Bible and an escapist church'.

2.48   The Lambeth Conference of 1988 called for a 'dynamic missionary emphasis going beyond care and nurture to proclamation and service'. It combined the different emphases of mission: 'personal evangelism, nurturing disciples, practical caring and the struggle for justice are bound up together and belong together, just as we do in the Body'. The Archbishop of Canterbury argued for the same unity of the apostolic nature of the church in his address to the Kanuga 1995 conference on evangelism:

It is often said that mission reflects the broad sweep of God's loving concern for his world whereas evangelism has a more specific focus on the call to follow Christ. But it is a mistake to separate them too sharply. Mission which does not have evangelism as a sharp focus is not Christian mission, and evangelism which keeps itself aloof from matters of justice and human welfare does not reflect adequately the biblical revelation. 'We must insist on the seamless character of mission and evangelism.'[1]

This was taken further in the MISSIO Report of 1996 which urged the Anglican Communion to move beyond stereotypes into 'holistic evangelism'.

Kanuga specifically stressed the need for the training of lay evangelists, the emergence of shared total ministry and the training of clergy in evangelism, renewal and outreach (*The Cutting Edge of Mission*, p. 164).

The Resolutions of the 1998 Lambeth Conference do not make reference to the word 'Evangelist' as such, but Resolution II.6.c) expresses a determination that the impetus of the Decade of Evangelism should not be lost and states, 'The primary task of every bishop, diocese and congregation in the Anglican Communion is to share in and show the love of God in Christ Jesus – by worship, by the proclamation to everyone of the gospel of salvation through Christ, through the announcing of good news to the poor and the continuing effort to witness to God's Kingdom and God's justice in act and word and to do so in partnership with Christians of all traditions.'

Resolution II.8.c) calls for bishops to give a priority to the furtherance of ministry to children and young people and asks for 'teams of adults and young people in as many congregations as possible to be trained for holistic ministry to young people outside the church, so as to speak of God's love in Christ . . .'

2.49   While there is no Communion-wide pattern for the use of evangelists there is much evidence for their widespread use in countries such as

Sabah, Uganda, Myanmar, Ghana, Nigeria, East Africa, Sri Lanka, South Africa and West Malaysia. The Melanesian Brotherhood is a religious order of evangelists founded in 1925 (the Community of the Sisters of Melanesia was founded in 1970). USPG reports that evangelists are an established part of the ministry in Madagascar with the Bishop of Mahajanga being supported by eight evangelists and three clergy. In Malawi one evangelist with a bicycle assists one priest in covering 28 parishes. CMS says that many evangelists, particularly in Pakistan and East Africa, are recognized and financially supported primarily by the community in which they live rather than by any ecclesiastical commissioning.

2.50 It is also true that lay workers such as catechists and Mothers' Union workers are also commissioned to evangelize without being designated as evangelists – indeed, in some parts of Africa any attempt to separate pastoring and evangelizing would not be understood (though Church Army officers in Africa are still commissioned as evangelists).

2.51 A notable initiative was the consecration of nine missionary bishops in Nigeria in 1991, who were commissioned to begin work in areas where there was very little Christian presence.

2.52 At the same time some provinces report that they did not see the need for evangelists since mission is the work of the whole church. However, it is noticeable that it is in those areas where the church is growing that evangelists are recognized and there appears to be no consequent loss of missionary zeal on the part of other members of congregations.

2.53 Some evangelists from other parts of the Anglican Communion have come to England, often through mission agencies such as CMS, USPG and Crosslinks. Although they are usually officially employed as assistant curates they are sometimes called 'Parish Evangelists' in their parish (including some who have been Archdeacons or College Principals in their own country). Some have been here for some time – Jacob Ajetunmobi from Nigeria is now in his eleventh year. An evaluation of their ministry shows that they ask the acute questions, especially in their early months, they teach English Christians how to give their personal testimony, and give help in new styles of worship, particularly in the ministry of healing. Furthermore, 'they place a high value on prayer and spending quality time with people'.

Note to Chapter 2

1. Cyril C. Okorocha (ed.), *The Cutting Edge of Mission: A Report of the Mid-point Review of the Decade of Evangelism*, Anglican Communion Publications, 1996.

CHAPTER 3

The Work of an Evangelist

3.1   The working party was asked to examine the use of evangelists in the New Testament and in Christian history. We hoped that this would lead us to a definition of the word 'evangelist' that could give greater clarity when the subject was being discussed.

We found that surprisingly little work had been done on any theological exposition of the word 'evangelist' in the New Testament and even less on its occurrence and significance in the Christian tradition. Different members of the working party therefore undertook to research different historical periods to uncover the ways in which the word had been used and how the apostolicity of the Church had been expressed. We would not claim that this is an exhaustive examination; indeed, it is a subject that calls out for further investigation. We would merely point out that it may reflect something of the difficulty that the Church has sometimes had in encompassing the ministry of the evangelist.

3.2   As there is little existing published material on this subject, this chapter sets out some of the material we examined. It should be noted that it is a discussion of the word 'evangelist' and not a history of evangelism itself. It leads on to the definition of the word at which we arrived (in para. 4.3).

Evangelists and the gospel

I.   THE 'EVANGELIST' IN THE NEW TESTAMENT

3.3   The word 'evangelist' is used three times in the New Testament, at Acts 21.8, Ephesians 4.11, and 2 Timothy 4.5.

3.4   Acts 21.8

'Philip the evangelist' first appears as one of the seven chosen to serve the tables of the Jewish Christian community in Jerusalem (Acts 6.1-6). Although Acts tells us that this service of the tables (6.2) left the apostles free for the service to the word (6.4), Philip himself is among those scattered by persecution who 'went from place to place, proclaiming the word' (8.4). The Ethiopian eunuch to whom Philip proclaims the good news about Jesus and whom he baptizes (8.26-40) foreshadows 'the conversion of the Gentiles' (15.3) and the preaching of the gospel 'to the ends of the earth' (1.8).

3.5   Ephesians 4.11

'The apostles, the prophets, the evangelists, the pastors and teachers' are described as gifts of the exalted Christ to his Church. Together they carry out their work of service,[1] bringing individuals and the whole Church to maturity and completeness (4.12f). It has been suggested that in this letter the evangelists are presented as those who continue the apostolic preaching and founding of churches, and the pastors and teachers as those who now act as leaders of those churches in the place of the prophets.[2] However, the letter itself mentions only 'their work directed to the saints'.[3] Whatever their particular responsibilities, 'the evangelists, the pastors and teachers' are together depicted as Christ's generous gifts to his Church and his means of equipping it to become what it already is as the fullness of Christ (1.23).

3.62   Timothy 4.5

Timothy, a leader entrusted with responsibility for the worship, teaching and common life of a local church, is charged: 'always be sober, endure suffering, do the work of an evangelist, carry out your ministry fully' (4.5). These four imperatives seem to provide an emphatic summary of what has previously been said. The letter has already urged Timothy both to suffer and to teach for the sake of the gospel through which Christ brought life and immortality (1.8-14; cf. 2.8ff). It has connected the kind, gentle and patient conduct of a servant of the Lord with the success granted to his teaching (2.24f). It therefore seems likely that 'the work of an evangelist' is intended to embrace the whole of the charge 'to proclaim the message; be persistent whether the time is favourable or unfavourable; convince, rebuke, and encourage, with the utmost patience in teaching' (4.2). Again, it has been suggested that Timothy is expected to take the lead in proclaiming the good news to those outside the Church,[4] but it is certain that he himself is to remember the gospel – 'Jesus Christ, raised from the dead, a descendant of David' (2.8; cf. Romans 1.3f) – and to remind those inside the Church of this (2.14).

II.   THE GOSPEL

3.7   Although the word 'evangelist' is not used in the Greek translation of the Jewish Scriptures,[5] it is cognate both with *euangelion* (good news), used in 2 Samuel 4.10; 18.22,25, and with *euangelizesthai* (to proclaim good news), used most significantly in Isaiah 40-66, where the good news that God is coming to save his people is carried into effect by the messenger's proclamation (40.9; 52.7; 60.6; 61.1). This use of the Greek *euangelizesthai* to translate the Hebrew *basar* (to bring good tidings) helps us to understand that in the New Testament, too, the *euangelion* is the message of salvation and that the evangelist is the messenger who proclaims good news.

This is not the imperial *euangelion* of the birth, accession or victory of a Roman emperor proclaimed to a world that he is supposedly transforming.[6] Instead it is 'the good news of God's grace' (Acts 20.24; cf. 15.7), 'the gospel of your salvation' (Ephesians 1.13; cf. 3.6) and 'the gospel of peace' (Ephesians 6.15; cf. 6.19). 'Jesus Christ, raised from the dead, a descendant of David – that is my gospel' (2 Timothy 2.8), the gospel through which our Saviour Christ Jesus abolished death and brought life, and for the sake of which the messenger himself suffers (2 Timothy 1.8-11).

3.8   In Acts and 2 Timothy there are explicit connections between the evangelist and the gospel. Philip the evangelist proclaims 'the good news about the kingdom of God and the name of Jesus Christ' (Acts 8.12; cf.

8.25,40). The crowds hear what he says and see the signs he does (8.5-7), and Philip baptizes those who believe (8.12,38). It is fitting that he is a Jew, whereas they are Samaritans and a Gentile, since God himself proclaimed to Israel the good news of peace by Jesus Christ, revealing himself as Lord of all (10.36). Timothy's work as an evangelist includes his suffering and teaching for the sake of the gospel (2 Timothy 1.8-14) and his reminding the Church of the good news it has already heard (2.8-14). In Ephesians the connections between the gospel and the evangelists are implicit. The letter describes Christ's whole work of uniting Gentiles and Jews in himself as his proclamation of the good news of 'peace to you who were far off and peace to those who were near' (2.17; cf. 1.13) and it is as a servant of this gospel that Paul has been used to reveal the mystery that Jews and 'Gentiles have become fellow-heirs, members of the same body' (3.6f; cf. 6.19). It is consistent with this presentation of the proclamation of the gospel that the evangelists are included among those whose ministry strengthens the saints and builds up the body of Christ (4.11f). It therefore seems likely that when the readers are urged to put on their feet 'the preparedness of the gospel of peace' (6.15), this is their readiness for spiritual combat paradoxically provided by the gospel of peace rather than their readiness to proclaim the gospel.[7]

3.10   The three references to evangelists encourage us to understand their work as their proclamation of the good news and also remind us of the power of the gospel they serve. It is the good news proclaimed by God (Acts 10.36) and by Christ Jesus (Ephesians 2.17) as well as by the Church. It is grounded in the nature of God revealed in Jesus Christ – 'he is Lord of all' (Acts 10.36), and it creates the community that embodies the unity of God himself: 'one Lord, one faith, one baptism, one God and Father of all' (Ephesians 4.5f). The life that Christ brought to light through the gospel is shared by the apostle's announcing the good news and by his suffering and teaching for its sake and as its servant (2 Timothy 1.10-12; 2.8-10).

3.11 Elsewhere in the New Testament we are presented with the same pattern. In Mark, the good news is both told by Jesus (1.14f) and is to be told about Jesus (14.9), whose death and resurrection are proclaimed by the woman who anoints him at Bethany.

In heading his work 'The beginning of the gospel of Jesus Christ' Mark may have both meanings in mind (cf. 13.10).[8] It is for the sake of Christ and the gospel that his disciples must themselves be ready to lose even their lives to receive eternal life (8.35; 10.29). In Luke, Jesus declares the prophecy of Isaiah 61.1 to be fulfilled in himself: 'The Spirit of the Lord is upon me, because he has anointed me to bring good news to the poor' (4.18), and so again he both proclaims (4.43; 8.1; 20.1) and is (2.10; 7.22; 16.16) the good news of the reign of God. The twelve are themselves sent out by Jesus 'to proclaim the kingdom of God and to heal' (9.2), and from a careful comparison of the parallel accounts of the mission of the twelve (Matthew 10.5-15; Mark 6.6b-13; Luke 9.1-6) Martin Hengel concludes that: 'Jesus' call is uttered with an eye to the dawning rule of God and he brings the individual person who is called by him into a community of life and destiny with him, involving an absolute break with all ties, thus at the same time initiating him into service for the cause of the kingdom. This gives the Mission tradition in Mk and Q its necessary and fully justified sense. The disciples were to act for the dawning Rule of God with the same authority as their master who called them.'[9] In the post-Easter community the emphasis shifts from the good news first proclaimed by Jesus to the good news now proclaimed about Jesus. However, it should not be overlooked that these are held together in Matthew 28.18-20, in the risen Christ's great commission. Jesus' work of making disciples by bringing people into community with him and by teaching them is to be continued by the disciples who are now charged to baptize in the name of God, whose nature as Father, Son and Holy Spirit has been revealed.

3.12 Paul writes to the Corinthians about the good news that he proclaimed, that they received, in which they stand, and through which they are being saved (1 Corinthians 15.1f). Its content is what God has done in Christ, and it is briefly stated in 1 Corinthians 15.3-5 and, somewhat differently, in Romans 1.2-4. Paul describes this gospel as the gospel of God

(Romans 1.1),[10] the gospel of Christ (Romans 15.19),[11] and indeed as 'our gospel' (2 Corinthians 4.3; 1 Thessalonians 1.5; 2 Thessalonians 2.14) and 'my gospel' (Romans 2.16; 16.25; cf. 2 Timothy 2.8). In speaking of 'my gospel' Paul underlines his vocation to proclaim Jesus Christ to all the Gentiles (Romans 16.25f), as 'an apostle set apart for the gospel of God' (Romans 1.1; cf. 1 Corinthians 1.17; Galatians 2.15f). In defending this apostleship Paul seeks to show that his own life is shaped by the good news of the death and resurrection of Christ, that 'his adversities are to be understood as a dying that brings life' (see 2 Corinthians 4.7-15), and that his life 'is lived not for oneself but for Christ and in the service of others' (cf. 2 Corinthians 5.14-21).[12] When Paul urges that 'God is making his appeal through us', he stresses also that he is 'becoming the righteousness of God' (2 Corinthians 5.20), the ambassador who 'actually becomes the living embodiment of his sovereign'.[13] In proclaiming 'our gospel' Paul insists that 'we do not proclaim ourselves', but he equally insists that 'we proclaim Christ Jesus as Lord' and 'ourselves as your servants for Jesus' sake' (2 Corinthians 4.5). Paul's gospel is therefore the proclamation that both founds and builds up the community: God 'is able to strengthen you according to my gospel and the proclamation of Jesus Christ' (Romans 16.25). Those who confess this gospel stand in it (1 Corinthians 15.1) and are subject to it (2 Corinthians 9.13). Their faith and love may itself be proclaimed as good news (1 Thessalonians 3.6).

3.13   This brief study of the gospel that is proclaimed suggests that for the apostle Paul and his co-workers in evangelism (2 Corinthians 8.18; Philippians 4.3; cf. Colossians 1.7; 4.12), just as for Philip, Timothy and the evangelists in Ephesians, 'the work of an evangelist' is both proclamation and service, and that 'the work of the gospel' (Philippians 4.3) is for those outside and those inside the Church.

'Peace to you who were far off and peace to those who were near' (Ephesians 2.17)

I.   NOT FROM THE JEWS ONLY BUT ALSO FROM THE GENTILES
       (ROMANS 9.24)

3.14   Paul tells the Corinthians that one of his co-workers in evangelism, 'the brother who is famous among all the churches for his proclaiming the good news', has been appointed by the churches to travel with Paul with a particular responsibility for administering the collection for the church in Jerusalem (2 Corinthians 8.18f). This collection was intended not only to address the economic need of the poor (Galatians 2.10), but also to express the unity of Jewish and Gentile Christians. Since the Gentiles have received a share in the spiritual blessings of the saints in Jerusalem, they should be of service to them in material things (Romans 15.25-27; cf. 1 Corinthians 16.1-4; 2 Corinthians 8-9). The appointment of the unnamed brother is another example of the close connection between the proclaiming of the good news and the service of the saints. It is also a reminder of the fact that this proclamation of the good news about the death and resurrection of the Messiah according to the scriptures (1 Corinthians 15.3-5) was a message both for those who were God's people and for those who were not. It was proclaimed to all those whom God 'has called, not from the Jews only but also from the Gentiles' (Romans 9.24). The gospel was preached first to Jews, who 'were entrusted with the oracles of God' (Romans 3.2) and then to Gentiles, who 'turned to God from idols, to serve a living and true God' (1 Thessalonians 1.9).

3.15   Philip the evangelist was one of the group of Greek-speaking Jews from the Diaspora who joined the first Christians in Jerusalem. Stephen, the leader of this group, took a more negative view of the Temple and of the sacrifices prescribed in the Torah than did the Aramaic-speaking Peter and James (Acts 6-7). It is interesting to note that this difference of view already existed within Judaism, and that some of 'the Hebrews' among the Jewish Christians seem to have escaped the persecution of 'the Hellenists' that led to the death of Stephen and the expulsion of others, including Philip.[14] It was this expulsion that led to the proclamation of the good news to the Gentiles and the momentous decision to maintain within one Church a crucial 'distinction between Jewish Christian obedience to the law and Gentile Christian obedience to the Law'.[15] This preaching to the Gentiles meant that, while Judaism certainly attracted its adherents,[16] proselytizing mission was, on the other hand, crucial to the spread of Christianity'.[17] However, it must not be forgotten that Christianity began as a renewal movement within Judaism, and that its emergence as an identifiable separate entity was a gradual process. The first pagan author to refer to Christians as distinct from Jews is Pliny the Younger, writing in AD 112 (Epistle 10.96).

3.16   Michael Green rightly observes that 'the Christian faith grew best and fastest on Jewish soil, or at least, soil that had been prepared by Judaism'[18]. This point must warn us against too readily rebuilding in our proclamation a dividing wall between those who are far off and those who are near, and against too sharply separating the gospel for outsiders from the gospel for insiders. It is salutary to note that we cannot tell from the evidence whether the Roman consul Flavius Clemens, put to death by Domitian in 95AD (Dio, Hist 67.14; cf. Suetonius Domit 15.1), died as a Jewish sympathizer[19] or as a Christian.[20]

3.17   What is quite clear is that the work of an evangelist embraces easily both Philip's proclaiming to those outside and Timothy's reminding, by encouragement and warning, of those within.

II.   AS IT IS THEY ARE HOLY (1 CORINTHIANS 7.14)

3.18 In the first century AD there was a variety of ways in which sympathetic Gentiles could associate themselves with their Jewish neighbours, ranging from admiring some aspect of Judaism to being fully integrated into the community as proselytes.[21] Indeed, the New Testament itself identifies such individuals. We meet, for example: the centurion who is a friend of the Jews and built a synagogue (Luke 7.1-10); Cornelius, another centurion, who feared God[22] and gave alms to the people (Acts 10.1f); the Ethiopian eunuch, who had come to Jerusalem to worship and was reading the Jewish scriptures (Acts 8.27f); Timothy, who had a Jewish mother but had not been circumcized as a child (Acts 16.1-3); and 'Nicolaus, a proselyte of Antioch' (Acts 6.5).

3.19   Given its beginnings within Judaism it is not surprising that there is something of this variety of association also in relation to the Christian community. The pro-consul of the province of Cilicia, Sergius Paulus, seems only to have acknowledged the power of the God of Barnabas and Paul (Acts 13.12). Members of the household of a convert were some-times baptized with them (Acts 16.13-15, 29-34; 1 Corinthians 1.16). It is possible that the slave Onesimus was a member of such a household, since Paul writes to the church in 'the house' of his master Philemon and mistress Apphia (Philemon 2). But if Onesimus' first association with the Christian community was in the household, it is through his encounter with Paul, who became his 'father' (Philemon 10), that his life was trans-formed (Philemon 11). Paul also addresses the concerns of believers married to unbelievers (1 Corinthians 7.12-16). He contends that by the believer's continuing in marriage the unbelieving partner and the children are already 'made holy', the term he has used for the members of 'the Church of God in Corinth' (1 Corinthians 1.2; cf. 6.11; 1 Thessalonians 5.23). He also expresses to the believer the hope that 'you might save' your partner.

3.20   Christianity, rooted as it is in Judaism, seems always to have recog-nized some stages in association with the Church. This is not at all to deny the urgency of the appeal to 'repent and be baptized' (Acts 2.38), but it is a further explanation of the continuity we have identified between the proclamation to those outside and the proclamation to those inside.

The work of the gospel (Romans 15.16)

I.   EVANGELISM AND TEACHING

3.21   Luke describes how Jesus 'was teaching the people in the temple and telling the good news' (20.1), and in Acts he says of the apostles that 'every day in the temple and at home they did not cease to teach and proclaim Jesus as Messiah' (5.42; cf. 4.2). If the foundation is laid by the proclamation of what God has done in Christ in fulfilment of the scriptures (see, for example, Acts 10.34-43; 1 Corinthians 15.3-5), then the building must continue with teaching that brings to life the character of this Jesus, 'who went about doing good' (Acts 10.38) and 'who died for our sins . . . and was raised' (1 Corinthians 15.3f). The teaching will explain how all this is indeed 'in accordance with the scriptures' (1 Corinthians 15.3f) and how 'all the prophets testify about this' (Acts 10.43). And through this teaching there is the constant reminder of 'the foundation that has been laid: that foundation is Jesus Christ' (1 Corinthians 3.11).[23]

3.22 Evangelism and teaching therefore belong together, proclaiming and explaining Christ, in whom the promises of the Jewish scriptures are being fulfilled. The process began as Philip the Evangelist showed the Ethiopian eunuch that Jesus is the one about whom the prophet speaks (Acts 8.34f), and it continues as Timothy works as an evangelist, using the scriptures to ensure that the Christian people he leads are 'equipped for every good work' (2 Timothy 3.16f). Paul says of the whole process: 'you have become obedient from the heart to the form of teaching to which you were entrusted' (Romans 6.17), and in Acts commends the Ephesian elders 'to God and to the message of his grace, a message which is able to build you up and to give you the inheritance among all who are sanctified' (20.32).

3.23 The first letter of Peter expects every Christian 'always to be ready to make your defence to anyone who demands from you an accounting for the hope that is within you' (1 Peter 3.15). The Christian scriptures are themselves such a defence and account. Not only the epistles but also the gospels were written for believers in the first instance, enabling them to explain and defend their faith when the occasion offered. Matthew seems to be designed to encourage and strengthen the community of Jewish Christians and to equip them to reply to other Jews whether curious or critical.

Mark was written for the training of Gentile Christian disciples, to enable them to explain why Christians hold Jesus to be the Messiah and the Son of God.[24] The two volumes of Luke and Acts were written primarily as a work of edification for a Christian audience, encouraging them to see that 'God was truly at work in their movement, fulfilling his ultimate saving purposes for the nations'[25] and offering them thereby an account and defence for unbelievers. Even John, written to encourage its readers to believe that Jesus was the Messiah and the Son of God (20.31), 'was written by a Christian for Christians'[26] inspiring them to maintain their faith at a troubled time of separation from Jewish society. Although written for believers, all four gospels are nevertheless powerful tools in the hands of Christians willing to engage in Christian apologetic, giving an account and defence of their faith. The nature of the Christian scriptures is therefore in itself strong evidence for the intimate connection between teaching and evangelism.

II.   EVANGELISM AND SERVICE

3.24   Philip the Evangelist was first appointed to the service of the tables, just as Paul proclaimed Jesus Christ as Lord and himself as a servant. Timothy carried out the work of an evangelist and fulfilled his service, just as the evangelists in Ephesians carried out their work of service in building up the body of Christ.

3.25   Given this close connection between evangelism and service, it is not surprising that the ways in which the faith is commended to outsiders include honourable conduct (1 Peter 2.12), behaviour within a marriage (1 Peter 3.1f; cf. 1 Corinthians 7.12-16) and a community united in worship (1 Corinthians 14.24f). As Jesus himself sent out his disciples 'to proclaim the kingdom of God and to heal' (Luke 9.2; cf. Matthew 10.7f), so those who preach the good news of Jesus perform 'many signs and wonders' (Acts 2.43).[27] Paul too holds together the power of preaching and the power of signs and wonders: 'what Christ has accomplished through me to win obedience from the Gentiles, by word and deed' (Romans 15.18f; cf. 2 Corinthians 12.12). Above all, Paul holds together his proclamation of the gospel with his 'being given up to death for Jesus' sake, so that the life of Jesus may also be made visible in our mortal flesh' (2 Corinthians 4.11). It is entirely in line with Paul's teaching that in the Revelation to John the 'witnesses to Jesus' (17.6; cf. 2.13; 11.3) are the martyrs who by their faithfulness to 'Jesus Christ, the faithful witness' (1.5; cf. 3.14) proclaim that the slaughtered Lamb is indeed on the throne of God (5.6ff).

3.26   Gerd Theissen has suggested that there was a tension in the early Church between two types of preachers: the itinerant charismatics and the community organizers.[28] Within the New Testament this conflict is most evident in Paul's letters to the Corinthians, where Paul turns the charismatic poverty practised by the itinerants into a privilege, which he has renounced so that he 'may make the gospel free of charge' (1 Corinthians 9.3-18; cf. 2 Corinthians 11.7-11; 12.11-14). This tension is also evident in the Didache, where itinerant apostles and prophets (11-13) feature alongside resident bishops and deacons (15). This tension serves as a further reminder that there was no one pattern of ministry in the early Church, although the Didache notes that the 'bishops and deacons . . . also perform the service of the prophets and teachers' (15), and mentions only a ministry to the Church in both cases. Above all the Didache stresses that those who teach the truth should do what they teach (11). All our witnesses therefore agree that those who preach the gospel should conform their lives to the gospel. Whether by the poverty of dependence on the community or by the poverty of renouncing the right to support, those who proclaim the good news must live as the servants of God and of his saints.

The work of an evangelist

3.27   There is thus a variety of structures of ministry in the early years of the Christian movement. Although the New Testament speaks of bishops (overseers), presbyters (elders) and deacons (servants), the first two seem to be interchangeable (compare Acts 20.17 with 20.28, and see

Titus 1.5-7 and 1 Peter 5.1-4), and we also hear of other patterns, for example of 'apostles, prophets, and teachers' (1 Corinthians 12.28), whose work is perhaps continued by 'the evangelists, the pastors and teachers' of Ephesians (4.11). Since there are various patterns of ministry attested in the New Testament, and given that the rare occurrences of the term 'evangelist' are found in three documents that emerged at different times and in different contexts, we cannot clearly define what the New Testament means by the word 'evangelist'. However, we have seen that the term can embrace those in Ephesians whose work is described only by its influence on the Church (4.12f), Timothy whose responsibility for the Christian community includes a concern for the opinion of outsiders (1 Timothy 3.7; 6.1), and Philip, who both serves the Christian fellowship (Acts 6.2) and proclaims good news to the world. We can at least say that the New Testament encourages us towards a holistic definition of the word.

3.28 It is clear from the New Testament that the proclamation of the gospel is central to the life of the Church. 'The work of an evangelist' is therefore to be undertaken by all those with a particular charge for over-sight, teaching and service in the Christian community, so that all God's people may proclaim the good news of God in Christ. The recognition and encouragement of those with special gifts for different aspects of the work of mission and evangelism is integral to the Church's call to com-mend all the world 'to God and to the message of his grace, a message that is able to build you up and to give you the inheritance among all who are sanctified' (Acts 20.32).

The use of the word 'evangelist' in Christian history

3.29 The working party found that there had been little investigation into what the word 'evangelist' meant during the history of the Church. This section therefore seeks to outline the results of investigations made by individual members of the working party into different periods of Christian history (we are also much indebted to Dr Lionel Wickham of

Cambridge for comments on the patristic period). Once again we would emphasize that this is not a history of evangelism but an outline of the use of the word 'evangelist'.

I.   THE EARLY CHURCH

3.30   The apostles were known for their evangelistic enterprise as the traditions about the mission of St Thomas to India and St Andrew to Scythia testify. Evangelism was linked with the apostolic ministry and subsequently with the ministry of a bishop.

3.31   However, no specific office of Evangelist is known in the Church within the era of the Church Fathers — nor was there any office of Catechist, though the minor orders of Reader, Exorcist, etc. are mentioned at least as early as the third century. The word evangelist appears to be used only as a description of the writers of the four gospels (St Mark the Evangelist, etc.). The reason for this may well be the context in which the Church was set. Before the peace of Constantine, the Church was at best a tolerated institution and at worst subject to bouts of anti-Christian agitation and occasional Imperial attempts at suppression such as that under Diocletian. The Church therefore had few opportunities for overt evangelization, though there were examples of those, such as Gregory the Illuminator (c. 240-332), who found their faith when they were away from their native land and then returned home to establish the church.

3.32   Generally the Christian faith was spread through personal contact and through the writings of the apologists who explained the faith and countered the arguments of their opponents. The ordinary citizens of the Roman Empire would have become aware of the existence of a local Church through its good works in caring for the needy within the church and, to some extent, those outside it. The Christians were also sufficiently confident in their way of life for Minucius Felix to say that such 'beauty of life . . . encourages strangers to join the ranks' (Oct. 31.7). They might also be impressed by the conspicuous heroism of some of its members at times of persecution, or by displays of spiritual power, particularly exorcisms.[29]

3.33 With the coming of Constantine more open evangelism became possible and the word evangelist may have become more common as a description of those who proclaimed the gospel to those outside the church. Thus Eusebius in his *Ecclesiastical History* (c. 325) described the work of the missionary in words that could have been used of the ministry of St Paul. Speaking of some members of the post-apostolic church he writes:

> Their first action in obedience to the instructions of the Saviour, was to sell their goods and distribute them to the poor. Then, leaving their homes, they set out to *fulfil the work of an evangelist*, making it their ambition to preach the word of the faith to those who had yet heard nothing of it, and to commit to them the books of the divine Gospels. They were content simply to lay the foundations of the faith among these foreign peoples: they then appointed other pastors, and committed to them the responsibility for building up those they had merely brought to the faith. They then passed on to other countries . . . (III.37.2-3)

3.34 In 341 another Eusebius (of Nicomedia and Constantinople) consecrated Ulfilas, who had a Gothic mother, as missionary to the Goths. His long ministry beyond the boundary of the Roman Empire, during which he translated most of the Bible into the vernacular, led to the Goths being converted to (Arian) Christianity. A similar missionary bishop can be seen in Patrick, who was sent as 'bishop in Ireland'. Most of the evangelists of this period were monks like the Copts who worked in Ethiopia and the extraordinary workers of the Nestorian Church in Central Asia and China.

3.35 There was therefore precedent for the action of Gregory the Great in sending Augustine and his 40 companions to evangelize England in 597. This is only the most famous example of Church leaders setting aside individuals to evangelize areas that were perceived to be pagan. Often the person was consecrated as bishop before departure as in 597, and in 634 in the smaller expedition launched by Pope Asterius when he consecrated Birinus also to be an evangelist to England. While it is dangerous to argue from silence in a period when there is so little evidence, it does seem that it was normal that the chief evangelist and leader of an expedition would be a bishop, often consecrated especially for the task by the Pope.

3.36   The Celtic pattern was somewhat different. Celtic monasteries saw part of their ministry to be evangelization. The 'perigrinati' ('wanderers') were encouraged to leave their mother house to go into non-evangelized areas and establish new monasteries and bring the faith and baptism to their neighbourhood. Columbanus (d. 615) planted monasteries in France, Switzerland and Italy but he is only the best known of the monks, mainly from Ireland, who established scores if not hundreds of monasteries over much of the continent, St Gall and Bobbio among them.

3.37   Celtic monasteries were ruled by an Abbot or Abbess and sometimes a bishop and his team would be sent out for primary evangelization. Few names have come down to us from those shadowy times, most of those being bishops honoured by the churches they founded.

3.38   The Roman Benedictine Order was less prepared to let monks roam at will and the monastery as a means of evangelization became less significant as the Benedictine order became the norm for monastic life over much of Europe. By the end of the seventh century there seems to have been a mixture of both the Celtic pattern and also the more organized Roman expeditions. The Irish monasteries spread as far as Kiev and Poland in the East and Taranto in the South. Contemporaneously, expeditions were sent to the Frisians (under Willibrord, c. 690) and to Germany (under Boniface, c. 719): in both cases the leader went to Rome to receive the blessing and mandate of the Pope and to be consecrated for their task. These leading missionaries were often described as 'apostles'. However, the evangelistic zeal of the monastery was not finished. The rise of the mendicant orders in the thirteenth century gave a fresh impetus to mission. The friars, particularly the Dominicans and the Franciscans, were the primary evangelists of the growing urban populations of Europe and of the peoples beyond.

3.39   It can be stated as a broad generalization that in the West at this period the Roman Church saw the evangelization of the non-Christian world as a priority for which successive Popes took responsibility. The Celts on the other hand had very few 'campaigns' but saw their monasteries as the main means of mission as they spread like strawberry plants into non-Christian areas. However, in both traditions, the bishop was seen as the chief evangelist.

II.   THE REFORMATION

3.40   Calvin recognized the offices of apostles, prophets, evangelists, pastors and teachers (Ephesians 4.11), and saw the evangelists as 'closely allied in office, but inferior to an apostle'. He argued that neither apostles nor evangelists nor prophets were necessary after the initial phase of the Church's mission and they were subsumed in the office of the pastor. However, this was not absolute: 'I do not deny that the Lord has sometimes at a later period raised up apostles or at least evangelists in their place, as happened in our own day.'[30]

3.41   However, that reference is exceptional. In the post-Reformation period evangelism was not much countenanced by the national Protestant churches of whatever ecclesiology. The work of the Church was essentially pastoral, helping people to a deeper discipleship.

3.42   It appears that it was mainly in some Protestant circles outside the presbyterian and episcopal churches of the day, that the word 'evangelist' was used with its present connotations. In *Pilgrim's Progress* the first person that Christian encounters as he staggers from his home in search of salvation is Evangelist. It is he who helps him on his way, reprimanding him when he strays and guiding him to the 'little wicket gate'. Bunyan (1628–88) and his small Independent church in Bedford saw the evangelist as instrumental in helping people to faith. However this use of the word was not wholly confined to Independent circles. Thus we find Bishop Burnet of Salisbury saying in 1681 'that there should be in every diocese some who should go round a precinct and preach like evangelists'.[31]

3.43   In the sixteenth century and most of the seventeenth it was not the Protestant churches but the heirs of the Counter-Reformation who were at the forefront of missionary work. The Roman Catholic Church was sending missionaries to South America soon after its discovery, and they ventured far beyond the colonies of Spain and Portugal. The Jesuits began missionary work in India in 1542; St Francis Xavier went to Japan in 1549 and Matto Ricci and Michele Riggieri reached China in 1582.

3.44   It was not until much later that the churches of the Reformation began missionary work overseas and that was almost always the result of personal initiatives such as that of Thomas Bray and the four laymen who set up SPCK in 1698 and SPG in 1701. However, their intention was only to evangelize within the British colonies: it was the Moravians who determined to go to places where Christianity was not already established, and in the mid-eighteenth century they established missions in South Africa, Greenland and the West Indies.

3.45   The end of the eighteenth century saw a significant expansion of missionary work. The Methodist Missionary Society was founded in 1786, William Carey sailed to India in 1793 and CMS was founded in 1799. They received little encouragement from the churches that sent them, and it was not until the Evangelical Revival and the Tractarian movement in the Church of England that there was widespread support for missionary work from the Church hierarchy. Even in these circles the word 'evangelist' was not much used. CMS records show that 'Associate Evangelists' were appointed in India in 1888, but as late as the Report of the Edinburgh Conference of 1910 the word 'workers' was preferred to 'evangelist'.

3.46   The need for evangelists working within Britain rather than overseas was recognized first by the nonconformists: the Societas Evangelica for the training of evangelists was set up in 1776, though the word 'evangelist' only came into common usage in the next century through organizations such as Spurgeon's Society of Evangelists. The word was used widely by Anglicans during the same period and it is used in official reports from the 1860s onwards in discussions regarding the Office of the

Reader and the formation of the Church Army (in 1882). Since then it has been used frequently as descriptive of the ministry of certain individuals, such as the Revd David Watson and those who have worked with Springboard, and with such religious orders as the Society of St Francis. Mainly it has referred to those who have been well known for their preaching ministry.

3.47   In the USA the term 'evangelist' does not seem to have been much used until the advent of Charles Finney and his 'revivals' and the heroic work of the Methodist and Baptist preachers on the western frontier with their camp meetings and vast journeys (their life expectancy as an evangelist was four years). However, there is no doubt that it is mainly the excesses of some American evangelists that has led both to a dislike of the term 'evangelist', which is seen to imply a manipulative and simplistic ministry, and to a narrowing of his or her role to that of the preacher.

3.48   In sum it can be said to be surprising that a term that is mentioned three times in the New Testament should have almost disappeared from sight for so much of Christian history (except for its reference to the gospel writers). Its use seems to occur in times of considerable missionary expansion and to wither almost to nothing when either persecution or apathy curtails the expansion of the Church. Now it has surfaced again in the years christened by many denominations as The Decade of Evangelism. We would argue that it is a New Testament word, which needs to be rescued from caricature and honoured.

Notes to Chapter 3

1. See Andrew T. Lincoln, *Ephesians*, Word Books, 1990, pp. 253f, and Ernest Best, *Ephesians*, T.&T. Clark, 1998, p. 389.

2. See Lincoln, *Ephesians*, p. 250 and Rudolf Schnackenburg, *Ephesians: a Commentary*, T.&T. Clark, 1991, p. 181.

3. Ernest Best, *Ephesians*, Sheffield Academic Press, 1993, p. 47.

4. See George W. Knight III, *The Pastoral Epistles*, Wm B. Eerdmans, 1992, p. 457.

5. It is very rare outside Christian writings; see G. Friedrich, 'euangelistes' in G. Kittel and G. Friedrich (eds), *Theological Dictionary of the New Testament*, ET Wm B Eerdmans, 1964–76.

6. See G. Friedrich, '*euangelion*' in *TDNT*.

7. See Lincoln, *Ephesians*, p. 449.

8. See Morna D. Hooker, *The Gospel According to Mark*, A&C Black, 1991, p. 34 (on Mark 1.1) and p. 330 (on Mark 14.9).

9. Martin Hengel, *The Charismatic Leader and his Followers*, T.&T. Clark, 1981, pp. 87f.

10. See also Romans 15.16; 2 Corinthians 11.7; 1 Thessalonians 2.2,8,9.

11. See also 1 Corinthians 9.12; 2 Corinthians 2.12, 9.13, 10.14; Galatians 1.7; Philippians 1.27; 1 Thessalonians 3.2.

12. Steven J. Kraftchick, 'Death in us, life in you', in David M. Hay (ed.), *Pauline Theology*, Vol. II, Fortress Press, 1993, pp. 168 and 177.

13. N. T. Wright, 'On becoming the righteousness of God', David M. Hay (ed.), *Pauline Theology*, Vol. II, p. 206.

14. See Elisabeth Schussler Fiorenza, *In Memory of Her,* 2nd edn, SCM, 1995, pp. 162ff.

15. Richard Bauckham, *The Book of Acts in its Palestinian Setting*, Paternoster, 1995, p. 472.

16. See Irina Levinskaya, *The Book of Acts in its Diaspora Setting*, Paternoster, 1996, pp. 19–49: 'the sources from the first century do not support the view that there was large scale Jewish missionary activity' (p. 49).

17. Nicholas H. Taylor, 'The social nature of conversion in the early Christian world', in Philip F. Esler (ed.), *Modelling Early Christianity*, Routledge, 1995, p. 129.

18. Michael Green, *Evangelism in the Early Church*, Hodder and Stoughton, 1970, p. 28.

19. Thus Levinskaya, *The Book of Acts in its Diaspora Setting*, p. 8 and Taylor, 'The social nature of conversion in the early Christian world', p. 131.

20. Thus Green, *Evangelism in the Early Church,* p. 177.

21. See Taylor, 'The social nature of conversion in the early Christian world', pp. 129ff.

22. cf. Acts 13.16,26; 16.14; 18.7. In *The Book of Acts in its Diaspora Setting*, Levinskaya persuasively argues the accuracy of Acts' account of the existence of a category of God-fearers (p. 52ff).

23. See C. F. D. Moule, *The Birth of the New Testament*, 3rd edn, A&C Black, 1981, pp. 183ff.

24. Moule, *The Birth of the New Testament*, p. 93.

25. David Peterson, 'The motif of fulfilment and the purpose of Luke-Acts', in Bruce W. Winter and Andrew D. Clarke (eds), *The Book of Acts in its Ancient Literary Setting*, Paternoster, 1993, p. 104.

26. Barnabas Lindars, *John*, Sheffield Academic Press, 1990, p. 63.

27. cf. Acts 4.30; 5.12; 8.13; 14.3; Hebrews 2.3f.

28. Gerd Theissen, *The Social Setting of Pauline Christianity*, Fortress, 1982, pp. 27–54.

29. cf. Ramsay MacMullen, *Christianizing the Roman Empire*, Yale University Press, 1984.

30. Calvin, *Institutes* 4.3.4, p. 1057.

31. Bishop Burnet of Salisbury, *History of the Reformation*, Vol. II, 1681, p. 368.

CHAPTER 4

Evangelists – Do We Need Them?

What is an evangelist?

4.1   Having looked at the somewhat chequered career of the evangelist from New Testament times onward, the working party had no doubt that, however defined, the evangelist cannot be separated from the evangel that is entrusted to the Church. This means that the word must be defined holistically rather than more narrowly than the New Testament gives us warrant for.

4.2   We were conscious of the dangers of overly precise definitions of the term and in this we were helped by an examination of the use of the word 'evangelist' in Christian history. It was clear that the word had altered its meaning several times in the Christian tradition (cf. Chapter 3). We were also helped by realizing how difficult it is to give precise definitions to other New Testament ministries that are mentioned alongside that of the evangelist, such as apostle or prophet.

4.3   We therefore came to understand the word 'evangelist' as describing someone, man or woman, lay or ordained:

- who goes where the church is not;

- who proclaims and lives the gospel: the way in which this 'proclamation' takes place is essentially contextual, and is by no means limited to preaching or even to verbal communication;

- who interprets the Church to the world and the world to the Church;

- who comes from the centre of the Church and feeds from its riches and is accountable to it as well as challenging it;

- who encourages the whole Church in its work of evangelism, not least by communicating the gospel to those inside as well as outside the Church.

The debate about evangelists

THE IMAGE OF THE EVANGELIST

4.4   We found that it was impossible to discuss evangelists and their ministry without confronting the images portrayed in the media and the common perceptions within the Church. Without this, emotional responses cloud judgment.

4.5   The evangelist nearly always gets a bad press. In the media he (it usually is a he) is depicted as loud and insensitive, overintense, humourless and manipulative. It is the image of the pushy salesman. It is not an attractive picture and, as we met evangelists around the country, we realized that the caricature was very different from these humble men and women of God who simply had a desire to communicate a faith that had come to mean so much to them, and who longed to see others enter into a relationship with God.

4.6   There are also five perceptions within the Church that must be faced.

(a) The first suggests that evangelists are people who are difficult and uncooperative – lone rangers who brook no authority and 'do their own thing'. There is an element of truth in this – as can be seen in the definition in paragraph 4.3, part of the ministry of an evangelist is to challenge the Church. The evangelist proclaims the gospel, and that is always uncomfortable. He or she also seeks to interpret the world to the Church, and often the Church finds that daunting, as it is faced by the realities of the context in which it is set. But that is precisely why the Church needs the evangelist – as a spur to the Church to lift its eyes off its own concerns. Not surprisingly, evangelists sometimes feel that the Church is not listening. We found diocesan evangelists longed to be accepted and used by the Church and to receive any support and training that was offered.

(b) All evangelists are evangelicals. As a matter of fact we found that this was simply not true. All traditions within the Church were well represented in the people we met.

(c) Evangelists are preachers. In communicating the gospel many different means are used, and preaching is one that is God-given. A comparatively small number of the evangelists we met saw themselves as preachers: most of them were visiting, leading groups, encouraging the young, praying and sitting alongside people.

(d) Evangelists travel. The image is of someone who is footloose and rootless. Those diocesan evangelists who had a ministry across their diocese were naturally not in their parish church every Sunday, but we found a deep desire by the great majority of evangelists to be part of a parish church that would accept and support their ministry and from which they could feed.

(e) Evangelists knock on doors or preach on street corners and embarrass people. The ministries of the evangelists we met seldom involved the first and never the second. Most ministered through friendship and Christian nurture, through church planting and initiating work among the sick and the homeless, the young and those outside the Church.

4.7   Only as the Church rids itself of these inaccurate pictures can it fully use the ministry that is vital to its wellbeing. There were some who felt that the word was so loaded with unhelpful baggage that words other than 'evangelist' were best used. Others feel that the word is scriptural and can be rescued from public perceptions by sensible people showing that the ministry is one of love and service. The important thing is the reality of the ministry rather than what it is called.

THE DEBATE

4.8   We were not debating whether or not the Church of England should have evangelists. It has had them for over a century in the officers of the Church Army and has an increasing number of recognized diocesan evangelists.

4.9   The need for evangelism is also not at issue: when the committee of the Upper House of Canterbury reported in 1896 it noted: 'it will be generally admitted that a very large number of the people of this country are out of touch with the Church and indifferent to her worship in any form whatever'. A century later we can but echo the same words.

4.10   The question at issue, therefore, is not whether the Church should have evangelists but whether this ministry should be further encouraged and, if so, what form of recognition would be appropriate.

4.11   Three questions came to the forefront.

(a) *Does the recognition of evangelists mean that the responsibility of all the baptized to evangelize is thereby diminished?*

Some feel that this is so and that congregations will leave evangelism to the 'specialist'. If the caricature of the evangelist given above represented reality, this might be the case. However others think that, using the definition of evangelist we have given in paragraph 4.3, the evangelist will stimulate thinking, prayer and action in congregations; indeed, some incumbents of parishes that have evangelists report that this is the case. In particular, part of the work of an evangelist is to help the Church and individual Christians to tell the story of their own experience of God.

(b) *If we recognize evangelists by name shall we also have to recognize everyone from those involved in the healing ministry to those who deliver the parish magazine? Allied to this question is another: we live in an age that looks for recognition and within an education system that encourages it – should the Church resist this or accept it?*

It is true that in recent years there has been a great growth in diocesan educational schemes from Bishop's Certificate courses, to Pastoral Assistant Schemes, Lay Ministry Training and the like. On the one hand, it would be hard to suggest that the pastoral ministry of a congregation is diminished by having one or two Pastoral Assistants or, on the other, that their recognition opens the floodgates to everyone looking to be recognized by the bishop. It is not likely that a wider recognition of the scriptural ministry of the evangelist would be different. The growth of collaborative ministry through local teams within churches suggests that complementary gifts of ministry are needed, and that this should include that of the evangelist.

(c) *Can clergy be evangelists?*

It is argued that the ministry of the clergy is pastoral, caring for people and helping them in their spiritual lives. Others would respond that the ministry of the clergy is far wider than this and included in it is the responsibility of leading people from unfaith to faith: indeed, it can be argued that this is one of the main elements in spiritual direction. The ministry of baptism is mainly theirs and this sacrament is about entrance into the Kingdom of God. Bishops are told at their consecration that their duty includes the promotion of the mission of the Church 'throughout the world' (ASB). Clergy have the duty of seeking to bring people to Christ and this will be evangelistic. Some of them will be particularly gifted as evangelists and this may need to be recognized and used.

The words used to describe affirmation within the Church

4.12   From the start, the working party had difficulty with words. The Church of England affirms people with a rich variety of expressions, some of which we found bewildering. We also found that some commonly used words had a more restricted legal usage. There is a need for an Anglican glossary, for misunderstandings can arise when words are being used with different meanings by different people.

In the end we came to accept the following definitions, and have tried to follow this usage in our report.

4.13   *Ordination*

Refers to those who have been ordained bishop, priest or deacon.

4.14   *Admission to an Office*

The history of the usage of the word 'office' seems unclear. It was certainly in use in the nineteenth century and was used of the Office of a Lay Reader. Subsequently it was used of Evangelists and possibly Accredited Lay Workers. Candidates are admitted to an office. (The popular word is 'commissioned' but this is inaccurate.) Under Canon E 7.2 it is open to laymen and women to be admitted to the Office of an Evangelist.

4.15   *Accreditation*

This word is used widely to denote any form of recognition. However, it is also used more narrowly to describe only those who have been sponsored by a bishop, have been selected, and then trained at an 'accredited' college or course.

4.16   *Licensing*

This is the granting of an official permission by a bishop to fulfil a particular ministry, and applies both to clergy and laypeople. Thus, a bishop could license either a cleric or a layperson as an evangelist in his diocese under Canon C 12.

4.17   *Validation*

This word is used loosely to denote acceptance of an individual, but it more accurately describes the fulfilling of certain (usually legal) conditions.

4.18   *Commissioning*

This is widely used to describe any affirmation (usually in public) of someone whose ministry is being recognized, but should more strictly be restricted to the giving of authority by one person to another.

4.19   *Recognition*

This seems to have no overtones and is the word used in this report to describe any form of affirmation.

The place of the Church Army evangelists

4.20   The Church Army has had long experience of evangelists and their relationship to the rest of the Church. We drew heavily upon their experience and spent a day with their senior staff. We were impressed by their openness to new ideas and willingness to act as servants of the Church in sharing the lessons they had learned and the resources they had developed.

4.21   Two caveats need to be entered. Church Army officers are paid and they have been admitted into the Office of an Evangelist. The great majority of diocesan evangelists are unpaid and none of them are holders of that Office.

4.22   We considered the possibility of diocesan evangelists being admitted to the Office of an Evangelist in the same way as Church Army officers. However, we concluded that this would not be appropriate at this time for the following reasons.

(a) Previous attempts to take this path had foundered on the complexities involved, as the Gloucester Report of 1985 had shown.

(b) The newly founded College of Evangelists had gone down the route of straightforward recognition and it would be confusing if diocesan evangelists took another.

(c) The idea of diocesan evangelists is still in its infancy and dioceses need the flexibility to experiment.

4.23   Some dioceses will wish to include Church Army officers as members of any scheme that involves the recognition of diocesan evangelists, and will want to welcome them as members of any diocesan fellowship. Their pattern of accountability will be rather different and they are stipendiary, but there seems to be no reason why they cannot be part of a diocesan pattern. However, other dioceses may wish to take a different view and this must be left to the discretion of the individual bishop.

4.24   If a diocese decides that Church Army officers should not be part of a diocesan evangelists scheme it will be important that the expertise of these officers is used, possibly in the training of diocesan evangelists. This should not cause difficulty, any more than the fact that not all officers will be part of the national College of Evangelists. It certainly should not be seen in any sense as reflection upon them – dioceses vary as do the skills of individual Church Army officers. Further, they are in a different position from that of a voluntary worker in a diocese or parish: indeed, it can be argued that they are already recognized through their admission to the Office of an Evangelist and through their licensing by the bishop.

CHAPTER 5

Selection and Training

5.1   There is the need for a suitable selection process for evangelists and for an appropriate formation that embraces theological, sociological and practical work to give a foundation for their ministry.

Even if those who are to be recognized are already ordained there may well be a need for some further training before they can receive wider recognition. (In the dioceses we were in touch with there was an assumption that this is a lay ministry; we wish to question that assumption.)

5.2   The selection and training of diocesan evangelists will vary in accordance with the understanding of 'evangelist' that the diocese is following. There are three main systems.

(a) Where a few already experienced evangelists are being recognized, selection tends to be by interview with a Diocesan Missioner, a suffragan bishop or DDO. Approval by the PCC and an incumbent's reference are usually required.

Training is limited to those areas that seem to need attention and are adapted to the individual. In some examples we found that prospective evangelists have already been trained as Readers and just need extra training in missiology and the practice of evangelism. The same would be true of those who have been ordained. Sometimes modules from other training schemes are used, or the evangelist is asked to go on a course run by the Church Army, Springboard or similar organizations.

(b) Where an existing pattern of lay training is in operation, some dioceses invite as many as wish to join (usually subject to their PCC's approval and some financial contribution) to have two years of general training together and then to decide, usually in conjunction with a spiritual director or counsellor, upon their own gift towards the beginning of the third year. Where evangelists are concerned they then begin a year's specialized training.

(c) A collegiate style of training is being increasingly used in those parishes undertaking some form of lay team ministry (with or without an OLM). The team, including any possible evangelists, are chosen through the PCC and the incumbent.

In these cases members of the team are trained at parish or district level.

5.3   The areas that need to be borne in mind during any selection process for an evangelist are:

(a) a spiritual life founded upon a real experience of Christ in their lives, both in the past and in the present – this should be evidenced by a regular spiritual discipline and study of the scriptures;

(b) an enthusiasm for passing on the good news to others alongside a love and respect for people;

(c) a wish to be rooted in the local church even if God is calling him or her to a more itinerant ministry – this should be shown in an active life within a local parish church and a willingness to work with others under leadership;

(d) some understanding of the way in which the gospel relates to their own context at work and at home, and the ethical issues that arise;

(e) a warm and relaxed personality allied to a sense of humour. They should have shown themselves to be flexible in their approach to a wide variety of people and situations, and to have an understanding of failure in themselves and in others.

COMPETENCIES

5.4   It is useful for dioceses to have a checklist to see the areas in which lay or clerical evangelists need to have training. In the modern jargon these are the desirable 'competencies'.

5.5   Thus it is likely that well-equipped evangelists will have training in:

(a) the Bible, so that they will continue to be surprised by the scriptures and handle them with assurance and be able to put passages into context;

(b) doctrine, with particular reference to missiology and inter-faith issues. They will also examine different evangelistic patterns to distinguish the underlying doctrines and philosophies;

(c) ecclesiology, with reference to the different traditions and patterns of church life and the doctrines and assumptions that lie behind them. He or she will also have experience of different traditions within the Church of England and of other denominations;

(d) those sociological studies that give an awareness of cultural values and cross-cultural issues. He or she should also be conversant with current thinking about the sociology of religion;

(e) church history, with particular reference to the history of mission;

(f) communication skills, including the use of the modern media;

(g) sufficient adult education skills to enable the evangelist to be able to teach those within the church;

(h) human behaviour, with particular reference to faith development and the formation of a mature Christian;

(i) practical experience of different patterns of mission, ranging from those that are primarily pastoral to those that are more directly evangelistic;

(j) opportunities to experience different forms of evangelism under the supervision of a competent practitioner;

(k) above all they will be trained in the practice and discipline of prayer and continuing study.

Resources

5.6   There are a number of training resources outside the dioceses that are sometimes used. These are as follows.

(a) **The Church Army**

Modules that have been used for training by a number of dioceses already exist. In some cases these have been modules already in existence for the academic accreditation (from Leeds University via the College of Ripon and York St John) of students at the Church Army College. Some diocesan evangelists have found these to be too academic, and if there is not to be any academic accreditation this may possibly be the case. On the other hand, others have spoken highly of them: probably much depends upon the object of the training as seen by the individual evangelist and also upon his or her enthusiasm in approaching learning. Nevertheless, it may well be appropriate for the Church Army to discuss with diocesan missioners and some evangelists the appropriate subjects and approach that any such course should adopt.

The College at Sheffield has excellent resources and the possibility of distance learning should be explored; indeed, the Church Army Statement of Policy has already suggested this as a possibility. It is noticeable that the dioceses that have used the Church Army resources have generally been geographically adjacent to Sheffield or Blackheath – this is a severe limitation.

The Church Army College may also need to examine the nature of the students it takes at present. Virtually all of them now expect to be stipendiary Church Army officers at the end of their training and the Church Army then helps them to find suitable posts.

However, there may be a place for a further extension of Church Army training in two other directions:

- the holding of residential courses in Sheffield for evangelists who may not intend to become Church Army officers, or even to be stipendiary. This might well be attractive to some of the enthusiastic diocesan evangelists. These evangelists would appreciate the training given by the college and would come for a residential period;

- the non-residential training of potential Church Army officers. In the same way that non-residential training is increasingly significant for the ordained ministry, so there may be a case for the training of Church Army officers while they continue to be employed.

(b) **Other colleges and courses**

Cliff College provides a similar training to Church Army and although it is a Methodist foundation a number of Anglican evangelists attend its residential courses. In the same way, the London Bible College is used by those other than Baptists.

An increasing number of theological colleges and courses are providing distance learning in theological and other studies. Sometimes these extension studies include modules on evangelism. Many of these are fairly new and it is too soon to evaluate them.

(c) **The religious orders**

Several religious orders regularly conduct missions and frequently include others in their teams.

(d) **Springboard**

Springboard has increasingly seen itself as a training institution and its 'long courses' (two weeks of teaching and practice) have been used by several dioceses. It has also been involved with Post-Ordination Training and CME in a number of dioceses.

(e) **Voluntary organizations**

Organizations such as CPAS have had programmes for the training of evangelists for some time. The 'Arrow' course has been found useful.

(f) **Evangelists**

It has often been found that apprenticeship to an experienced evangelist can help a potential evangelist to see the opportunities and pitfalls of evangelism more clearly than any other form of training.

(g) **Overseas experience**

Many have found that one of the best training grounds is in the church in Africa or Asia where the vitality and newness of Christian faith has shown new horizons and new possibilities. Visits from this country through diocesan links, mission agencies such as USPG and CMS, or organizations such as SOMA have led to a number of clergy and laity learning much and discovering their evangelistic gifts.

Addresses of some of the available resources are given in Appendix C.

CHAPTER 6

Questions for Further Consideration

6.1   The recognition of lay and ordained evangelists within the Church of England outside the ranks of the Church Army is still at such an experimental phase that it would be entirely wrong for this report to suggest that there is any blueprint that can or should be universally adopted. It is too early to make judgments about the different approaches, though it is hoped that the questions posed in this chapter will help dioceses to choose the model that best suits their context.

The different social and ecclesiastical settings of the 44 dioceses militate against uniformity. Indeed, the reverse is true: we have found that the relative autonomy of the different dioceses has led to a wealth of different approaches that are of great value in acquiring experience, which can be helpful to other dioceses seeking to encourage the ministry of evangelists.

6.2   In this chapter we are only offering suggestions: we have not even christened the chapter 'guidelines' because that can suggest a preferred way of working. The subject can best be approached through a series of questions, which we believe need to be addressed by those who wish to consider the issue.

6.2.1 What definition of evangelist do you wish to work with?

This must be fundamental. Just to define evangelism is not enough – the Church does not define the work of a priest by describing the whole ministry of the Church, nor of a teacher by reference to educational theory. In the same way, the work of an evangelist is not established merely by delineating evangelism. The converse is also true: it is possible to have a definition of the ministry of an evangelist without having a precise definition of evangelism – just as you can define the work of a teacher without having an agreed theory of education. This does not mean that we should cease seeking to define evangelism more closely, but it does mean that we should not use the difficulties of missiological accuracy as an excuse to beggar ourselves by failing to recognize and use the evangelists that God has given to the Church.

We have suggested a particular approach to this question of defining the evangelist in Chapters 3 and 4 but we are all too well aware that this question has not been widely addressed in the Church. Indeed, perhaps it is because the Church has not looked closely enough at this issue that the deeply unattractive caricature of the evangelist has been established in many people's minds.

It is as this essential spadework is done that clearer views of the ministry of evangelism that would be most valuable in a diocese begin to emerge. Experience shows that when this is done, particular individuals who clearly already fit that ministry or those who might be appropriate after training begin to be identified.

6.2.2 **Which model of evangelistic ministry is right for your diocese?**

In paragraph 1.16 three types of recognition that are being used in different dioceses were described. In brief, these are:

- recognition of an existing ministry for those who have a proven track record as an evangelist;

- training for potential ministry for those who are selected for training as an evangelist;

- collaborative ministry where an evangelist is part of a 'local ministry team' made up of people of differing gifts.

These are not mutually exclusive for while the first is likely to be used primarily for those with a diocese or deanery-wide ministry the last two will be appropriate for those who work largely within their own parish. It is possible to envisage that a handful of people could be recognized as Diocesan Evangelists and many more as Parish Evangelists. Alternatively, they might all be described as Diocesan Evangelists but their sphere of operation could differ according to individual gifts and circumstances.

Dioceses that have already recognized evangelists recommend that in the early stages at least the greatest possible degree of flexibility should be retained.

6.2.3 **What degree of accountability is required?**

In those dioceses that already have diocesan evangelists working outside their own parishes some form of mentor is often appointed who can support and advise the evangelist. Where evangelists work within the parish, the parish priest is looked to primarily for encouragement and guidance since it is he or she who will be aware of the work of the evangelist and of his or her home background. However, someone outside the parish could also be available as a link with the diocese – some have appointed a 'Warden of Evangelists'.

What must not happen is a lack of accountability. By definition evangelists are working at the boundaries and often find themselves in unusual, challenging and sometimes discouraging circumstances. Many spoke of finding their ministry spiritually draining. They need help and encouragement and occasional checking from someone who has a real care for them as people and an equal passion for evangelism. Sometimes a support group can be set up to fulfil part of this task, but ultimately an evangelist cannot easily be responsible to a committee: there should be an individual who fulfils that role. This might well be a responsibility delegated by the bishop to someone such as the Diocesan Missioner or a Warden of Evangelists.

Where clergy are recognized as evangelists they will need to have their individual support and accountability structure.

6.2.4 **Should there be an agreement between the evangelist and the diocese or parish?**

The church already has much experience of arrangements with voluntary workers through good practice where Readers, Pastoral Assistants, etc.

are concerned and this expertise can be drawn upon. It is often found helpful to have an understanding, preferably written, of what the mutual expectations of the evangelist and the diocese or parish will be.

While these written agreements can seem to be unduly bureaucratic in flavour, experience has shown that they can prevent many problems arising and can give a sense of affirmation to the evangelist concerned. Since an evangelist may well be working in areas outside the normal work of the Church it can easily happen that their ministry is largely unknown to the congregation (an occasional report to them is found to be helpful).

Whether the evangelist is working primarily within their own parish or not, the matters that should be included in any agreement are: areas of ministry, training, standards of behaviour and accountability.

(a) *Areas of ministry*

There should be an outline of the areas of work that the evangelist may tackle, and the time that he or she can give to it.

There is always the danger that an evangelist ranges too widely and too thinly – never being able to finish work that has been begun: the importance of giving time to follow-up should be stressed. Evangelists are also always in danger of having too many demands made of them and the boundaries of their work need to be delineated.

It is often found that it is best if the amount of time promised at the beginning is the minimum. It is easier to increase from a low baseline than to excuse oneself from being unable to manage an overambitious schedule.

(b) *Training*

What further training is required? This may be academic or experiential, e.g. attendance at a Springboard course or a module at a university. Spiritual needs should be included and retreats and quiet days may well be in the agreement.

(c)   *Standards of behaviour*

A Code of Conduct or some similar delineation of the expected standards of behaviour can be attached to the agreement. A suggested model is set out in Appendix A.

The diocesan evangelist is a representative of the diocese and the parish and any shortcomings will reflect on these.

(d)   *Accountability*

It should be made clear exactly who the person is to whom the evangelist is responsible and the support structure that will be put in place. The spiritual and physical demands upon an active evangelist are great and the care given by the parish and diocese should reflect this.

6.2.5 What should be the obligations of the Church to the evangelist?

If there is to be an agreement setting out the position of the evangelist towards the Church then there should be a second section that sets out the obligations of the Church towards the evangelist.

The working party felt strongly that the obligations upon the Church should be as firm as those upon the the evangelist for there should be mutual responsibility. We have therefore put, in Appendix B, a Code of Conduct for the Church in relation to the evangelist, which should be taken as seriously as the Code of Conduct in Appendix A. Matters that could be included in an agreement are: diocesan and/or parish support, training, finance, publicity and family.

(a)   *Diocesan and/or parish support*

A clear description of the support structure to be provided should be detailed.

> A written statement is especially important in this area: personnel change, misunderstandings can occur, disciplinary matters occasionally arise, promised support given verbally can evaporate. In particular, there should be one named person appointed by the bishop, perhaps

a 'Warden of Evangelists', to whom the evangelist is responsible and who has the task of ensuring that what has been promised is delivered. There should also be an indication of the frequency of one-to-one meetings and of the availability of this person at other times.

There should be an indication of the degree of freedom of action the evangelist is to be given – can he or she take initiatives on his or her own? What limit is there on sums of money that may be spent? What degree of cooperation is expected with other leaders in the church?

(b) *Training*

There should be an indication of what further training is expected and who will pay for it.

(c) *Finance*

There should be a clear indication of the way in which expenses are to be paid.

Evangelists are often loath to indicate to parishes they visit what their out-of-pocket expenses are. It should not be their responsibility to ensure that these are met.

(d) *Publicity*

Even if evangelists are working mainly in their own parish they need invitations to exercise their ministry. It should be indicated who is responsible for publicity and what form it should take.

(e) *Family*

Care for the evangelist's family is always important but is of particular significance in the case of an evangelist working outside his or her own parish where the individual circumstances may not be as well known to the parish priest.

6.2.6 **What form of recognition should be given to the evangelists?**

The discussion in Chapter 4 gives some of the background to this question and some indication of why different dioceses might have different answers.

In thinking this through the diocese, under the guidance of the bishop, will need to take into account the other voluntary lay ministries that are recognized in the diocese and how the evangelists would fit into the pattern. Where there is a diocesan parochial lay ministry scheme (whether or not it is linked to OLMs) the possibility of recognizing the evangelists in the same way as the other ministries must be an obvious answer to the question unless the evangelists are to have a wider than parish ministry.

At present, considerable changes are taking place in the way in which the Office of a Reader is regarded and further discussions are taking place on the diaconate. It may be wise to retain a certain flexibility so that the position of the evangelist can be part of these wider considerations.

Since the bishop is the source of recognized ministry in an episcopal church there must be some way in which he can be brought into the process of recognition: this does not need to be by his physical presence but can be by letter or by someone delegated to represent him.

6.3   In this experimental period much can be learnt from other dioceses who have sought to answer the same questions. The working party found they were only too ready to give generously of their experience to others.

6.4   So far diocesan schemes have grown up piecemeal in response to local situations. It is hoped that this report will lead to growing cooperation between dioceses. This may also help in evaluation and may in time lead to a common approach to selection and training, such as has evolved in the history of the Office of Reader. This, in turn, will make it easier for one diocese to accept the recognition given by another. It is expected that the Board of Mission will have a central role in liaison and networking.

CHAPTER 7

Recommendations

The nature of this report means that it should be taken as a whole and these recommendations should not be regarded as a resumé.

Recommendations to the Church of England

7.1   During this period when the recognition of diocesan evangelists is still at an early stage in the Church of England we recommend that the Board of Mission should continue to act as a source of information and to monitor the progress of its development on behalf of the General Synod. It could do this first, by collecting and making available material used for the selection, training and use of evangelists, second, by arranging occasional conferences of those engaged in this field, and third, by bringing the subject before the General Synod when appropriate (paras 1.15; 6.4).

7.2   There has been little theological or historical research on the use and significance of the word 'evangelist' in the Christian tradition. We recommend that some of the work outlined in Chapter 3 of this report should be carried further (paras 3.1; 3.29; 3.48; 4.2).

7.3   We recommend that the Church should recognize fully the experience and resources that the Church Army can offer and make the fullest possible use of them. It should look carefully at how it can best support the work of the Church Army so that it may draw upon its expertise for the training and encouragement of diocesan evangelists and others (paras 5.6a).

Recommendations to those with diocesan evangelists or considering the possibility of introducing them

7.4   We recommend that when the place of the evangelist is discussed the caricature that clouds judgement should be considered as well as the real theological and practical issues (paras 4.4–11).

7.5   We recommend that it should be possible for clergy as well as laypeople to be recognized as evangelists. We recommend that dioceses should consider how they can recognize, train and use appropriately the evangelistic gifts of clergy (paras 2.44i; 4.11).

7.6   We recommend that lay candidates for the ministry of a diocesan evangelist should undergo a selection procedure that looks for the qualities and experience outlined in paragraph 5.3. Similarly, their training should include the areas outlined in paragraph 5.5, subject to the local context. Clergy candidates should receive such training as is appropriate to their previous experience.

7.7   When parish teams and other forms of collaborative ministry are being established we ask that the importance of evangelism should be accepted and consideration be given to the possibility of the recognition of the role of the evangelist (para. 1.16.3).

7.8   In the training of evangelists and other lay ministries we recommend that the home parish is closely involved throughout the period of the training of their candidates (paras 2.11; 2.42; 2.44d).

7.9   We recommend that written agreements should be drawn up between evangelists and their parishes and/or dioceses, which emphasize that responsibility of each to the other, which is at the heart of our understanding of the mutuality of ministry (para. 6.2.4; Appendices A and B).

APPENDIX A

Code of Conduct
for Diocesan Evangelists

As Christians, born again by the Spirit of God, we must ensure that our message is incarnational, and that our lives speak as loudly as our words. We will therefore endeavour to work within the ethical framework outlined below.

Mandate

- We believe that God in his love seeks to reconcile the world to himself and to make Christ known to the people.

- We believe that God has called us to be evangelists with Christ and that he has equipped us by the Holy Spirit with particular gifting to fulfil that calling.

- We believe that our call to ministry is a call to service, and we will not be motivated by a desire for personal gain. Rather we embrace a sacrificial lifestyle of availability to the direction of the Holy Spirit.

Means

- Our methods must stem from a conviction of the need to incarnate the gospel, and a recognition that all of humanity is made in the image of God, with inherent value and dignity.

- In recognition of the dignity and responsibility given by God to humanity, we will avoid manipulation and coercion, acknowledging that we are fellow-workers with Christ himself.

- It is our commitment to work ecumenically with local churches of all denominations and we will not undermine the ministry of local church leaders.

- Our actions will display an awareness of the importance of differing contexts and culture.

- We will endeavour to ensure that those who become Christians as a result of our ministry are fully integrated into a local worshipping community.

- As servants of the God who is Truth, in integrity we will strive for absolute accuracy in our publicity and in the reporting of statistical data.

- We will maintain accurate and open financial records and avoid any misuse of money.

- We will seek to be efficient in administrative matters and extend Christian courtesy to all.

- We will endeavour at all times to maintain a lifestyle that reflects the gospel, living lives of moral purity and joy.

- We acknowledge that our families are a gift given to us by God, and we will be faithful in serving them and fulfilling our reponsibilities to them, giving them love, care, respect and time.

- We accept the oversight of the Church, recognizing our need for care and support and our need of accountability in ministry. We will seek to ensure that appropriate support is given to us and that we honour those who are in positions of leadership in the church.

- We will be faithful in prayer and Bible reading and seek further opportunities to enlarge our knowledge of the faith and to deepen our spiritual life.

Appendix B

Code of Conduct for the Church in Relation to Evangelists

If an evangelist is recognized by the Church there should be a mutual accountability by which the church supports the evangelist as someone gifted by God in the communication of the gospel. This will include:

- helping the whole church to honour and respect the evangelist and his or her particular ministry and informing the church so that it is aware of his or her work;

- encouraging both public and private prayer for the evangelist;

- ensuring that the church is aware of the particular gifts of the evangelist and that they are used to the full;

- providing clarity of accountability so that the evangelist knows to whom he or she is primarily responsible. There should be regular times for appraisal, and for discussion of the most appropriate forms of support;

- ensuring that the evangelist has a spiritual director, mentor, support group or similar means of encouragement, prayer and guidance;

- giving the evangelist the greatest degree of freedom so that, subject to the accountability structure that has been established, he or she is free to experiment and venture into new areas of ministry;

- providing suitable initial training and subsequent continuing opportunities for learning, together with appropriate funding;

- ensuring that all appropriate expenses are paid promptly;

- ensuring that the evangelist has sufficient time for relaxation and for his or her family. In particular, the evangelist should not be burdened by tasks within the life of the church that hinder his or her evangelistic ministry.

Appendix C

Resources

The details of organizations providing training resources that are listed in section 5.6 and elsewhere are as follows.

(a)   **The Church Army**
      The Church Army
      Independents Road
      Blackheath
      London SE3 9LG
      Tel: 020 8318 1226
      Fax: 020 8318 5258

      Wilson Carlile College of Evangelism
      50 Cavendish Street
      Sheffield S3 7RZ
      Tel: 0114 278 7020
      Fax: 0114 279 5863

      The Sheffield Centre
      Tel: 0114 242 7451

(b)   **Other colleges and courses**

Dioceses will normally have links with local Church of England Theological Colleges and courses and will be aware of the resources on offer. However, there are a number of colleges that offer modules on evangelism for study by extension. As these are subject to change and development, they are not listed here in detail, but Diocesan Training Officers or the equivalent are welcome to contact the Board of Mission.

Dr Anne Richards
Board of Mission
Church House
Great Smith Street
London SW1P 3NZ
Tel: 020 7898 1444
Fax: 020 7898 1431

The details for Cliff College and the London Bible College are as follows.

Cliff College
Calver
Sheffield S32 3XG
Tel: 01246 582 321
Fax: 01246 583 739

London Bible College
Green Lane
Northwood HA6 2UW
Tel: 01923 826 061
Fax: 01923 836 530

In addition, Spurgeon's College, in conjunction with Oasis, offers a Diploma in Church Planting and Evangelism. Details can be obtained from:

The Academic Registrar
Spurgeon's College
189 South Norwood Hill
London SE25 6JD

(c) **The religious orders**

Details of the Society of St Francis and the other religious orders can be found in *The Church of England Year Book*.

(d) **Springboard**

    Springboard Office
    4 Station Yard
    Abingdon
    Oxon OX14 3LD
    Tel: 01235 553 722
    Fax: 01235 553 922

(e) **Voluntary organizations**

    Church Pastoral Aid Society
    Athena Drive
    Tachbrook Park
    Warwick CV34 6NG
    Tel: 01926 334 242
    Fax: 01926 337 613

    The Melanesian Mission
    The Rectory
    2 Harpsden Way
    Henley-on-Thames RG9 1NL
    Tel: 01491 573 401
    Fax: 01491 579 871

(f)   **Evangelists**

In addition to those mentioned above there is:

> The Fellowship for Parish Evangelism
> c/o Church Pastorial Aid Society (see p. 75)

(g)   **Overseas experience**

The world mission agencies linked to the Board of Mission through the Partnership for World Mission are listed below.

- Church Army
- Church's Ministry among Jewish People
- Church Mission Society
- Crosslinks
- Inter-continental Church Society
- Mid-Africa Ministry (CMS)
- Missions to Seamen
- Mothers' Union
- South American Mission Society
- Society for Promoting Christian Knowledge
- United Society for the Propagation of the Gospel

The addresses can be found in *The Church of England Year Book*.

The details for SOMA are:

> SOMA – Sharing of Ministries Abroad
> PO Box 6002
> Heath and Reach
> Leighton Buzzard LU7 0ZA
> Tel: 01525 237 953
> Fax: 01525 237 954